ISBN 978-1-332-93936-7
PIBN 10440438

1 MONTH OF
FREE
READING

at

www.ForgottenBooks.com

By purchasing this book you are eligible for one month membership to ForgottenBooks.com, giving you unlimited access to our entire collection of over 1,000,000 titles via our web site and mobile apps.

To claim your free month visit:

www.forgottenbooks.com/free440438

English
Français
Deutsche
Italiano
Español
Português

www.forgottenbooks.com

Mythology Photography **Fiction**
Fishing Christianity **Art** Cooking
Essays Buddhism Freemasonry
Medicine **Biology** Music **Ancient**
Egypt Evolution Carpentry Physics
Dance Geology **Mathematics** Fitness
Shakespeare **Folklore** Yoga Marketing
Confidence Immortality Biographies
Poetry **Psychology** Witchcraft
Electronics Chemistry History **Law**
Accounting **Philosophy** Anthropology
Alchemy Drama Quantum Mechanics
Atheism Sexual Health **Ancient History**
Entrepreneurship Languages Sport
Paleontology Needlework Islam
Metaphysics Investment Archaeology
Parenting Statistics Criminology
Motivational

an abridged copy of a tract which had given offense, in
which every offensive sentence was corrected, and the
whole put into the handsomest style and dress possible.
After the emperor had perused the petition, he handed
it back without saying a word, and took the tract. Their
hearts now rose to God for a display of his grace. "O
have mercy on Burma! Have mercy on her king."

But alas! the time was not yet come. He held the
tract long enough to read the first two sentences, which
asserted that there is one eternal God, who is independent
of the incidents of mortality, and that beside him there
is no God; and then with an air of indifference, perhaps
disdain, he dashed it down to the ground. Moung Zah
stooped forward, picked it up, and handed it to the missionaries. Moung Yo made a slight attempt to save them by
unfolding one of the volumes which composed their present
and displaying its beauty; but his majesty took no
notice. Their fate was decided. After a few moments,
Moung Zah interpreted his royal master's will in the following terms:

"Why do you ask for such permission? Have not the
Portuguese, the English, the Mussulmans, and people of
all other religions, full liberty to practise and worship
according to their own customs? In regard to the objects
of your petition, his majesty gives no order. In regard
to your sacred books, his majesty has no use for them;
take them away."

Something was now said about brother Colman's skill
in medicine; upon which the emperor once more opened
his mouth, and said, "Let them proceed to the residence
of my physician, the Portuguese priest; let him examine
whether they can be useful to me in that line, and report
accordingly."

He then rose from his seat, strode on to the end of the hall, and there, after having dashed to the ground the first intelligence that he had ever received of the eternal God, his Maker, his Preserver, his Judge, he threw himself down on a cushion, and lay listening to the music, and gazing at the parade moving on before him.

As for the missionaries and their present, they were huddled up and hurried away without much ceremony. They passed out of the palace gates with much more facility than they had entered, and were conducted first to the house of Mya-day-men. There his officer reported their reception, but in as favorable terms as possible; and as his highness was not apprised of their precise object, their repulse appeared probably to him not so decisive as they knew it to be.

They were next conducted two miles through the heat of the sun and dust of the streets of Ava to the residence of the Portuguese priest. He very speedily ascertained that they were in possession of no wonderful secret which would secure the emperor from all disease and make him live forever; and they were accordingly allowed to take leave of the reverend inquisitor, and retreat to their boat.

At this stage of the business, notwithstanding the decided repulse they had received, they still cherished some hope of ultimately gaining their point. They regretted that a sudden interruption had prevented their explaining their objects to Moung Zah in that familiar and confidential manner which they had intended; and they determined therefore to make another attempt upon him in private.

The following day, early in the morning, they had the pleasure of seeing their friend Mr. G. coming to their

F

THE CHILDREN OF MISSIONARIES

THE INVOLUNTARY INHERITORS

OF THEIR PARENTS' SUFFERINGS AND REWARDS

THIS BOOK IS AFFECTIONATELY DEDICATED

BY ONE OF THEIR NUMBER

TO

THE CHILDREN OF MISSIONARIES,

THE INVOLUNTARY INHERITORS

OF THEIR PARENTS' SUFFERINGS AND REWARDS,

THIS BOOK IS AFFECTIONATELY DEDICATED

BY ONE OF THEIR NUMBER.

PREFATORY NOTE

IT is my purpose in the following pages to present a clear and consecutive story of my father's life, which may be justly said to form the main artery of the American Foreign Missionary Enterprise. In order to do this I have essentially re-written the Memoir which I prepared ten years ago for Anson D. F. Randolph & Co., and have endeavored to meet the requirements of the younger generation of Christendom. Free use has also been made of the personal reminiscences contributed by the fascinating pen of Mrs. Emily C. Judson to Dr. Wayland's noble and comprehensive Memoir, now out of print. The American Baptist Missionary Union possesses a very full collection of journals and letters, etc., which have been very carefully studied. It is a matter for sincere thanksgiving that these were spared and not consumed in the recent fire at Tremont Temple, as was understood by me when this book was first published.

E. J.

NEW YORK, 1894.

CONTENTS

BIRTHPLACE OF ADONIRAM JUDSON, MALDEN, MASS.

Adoniram Judson.

ADONIRAM JUDSON

CHAPTER I

EARLY YEARS. 1788–1809

THE traveler who visits Malden, Massachusetts, one of the picturesque suburban towns of Boston, may find in the Baptist meeting-house a marble tablet, bearing the following inscription:

IN MEMORIAM.
REV. ADONIRAM JUDSON.
BORN AUG. 9, 1788.
DIED APRIL 12, 1850.
MALDEN, HIS BIRTHPLACE.
THE OCEAN, HIS SEPULCHRE.
CONVERTED BURMANS, AND
THE BURMAN BIBLE,
HIS MONUMENT.
HIS RECORD IS ON HIGH.

The old wooden house embosomed among the trees is still pointed out as the birthplace of Adoniram Judson. His father, also named Adoniram, was a Congregational minister, born in Woodbury, Connecticut, in June, 1752. He was married November 23, 1786, to Abigail Brown, who was born at Tiverton, Rhode Island, December 15,

1759. Soon after his marriage he settled in Malden, Massachusetts, and here his eldest son, Adoniram, was born.

The boy was precocious and learned to read when he was only three years old. While his father was absent on a journey, his mother conceived the idea of teaching her child, in order that she might give her husband an agreeable surprise on his return. She succeeded so well that when his father came home he saluted him by reading a whole chapter in the Bible.

His affection for his father must have been deeply tinged with awe; for the elder Adoniram was a stern man, and very strict in his domestic administration. He was a man of decidedly imposing appearance, his stature being rather above the average. His white hair, erect position, grave utterance, and somewhat taciturn manner, together with the position he naturally took in society, left one somewhat at a loss whether to class him with a patriarch of the Hebrews or a censor of the Romans. He was through life esteemed a man of inflexible integrity and uniform consistency of Christian character. To the influence of such a father perhaps were due the stately courtesy that characterized Mr. Judson's social intercourse throughout his whole life, and the dignity of style which pervaded even his most familiar letters.

The family lived in Malden until Adoniram was about four-and-a-half years old. During that time his sister, Abigail Brown Judson, was born, to become the companion of his childhood and his life-long confidante. She recently died in Plymouth, Massachusetts, at the age of ninety-five. She remembered hearing her parents relate that when her brother was only four years old, he used to gather together the children of the neighborhood to play church, he officiating as minister; and that even then his favorite hymn was the one beginning, "Go preach my gospel, saith the Lord."

In January, 1793, the family removed to Wenham, Massachusetts, a village about twenty miles northeast of Boston, where Adoniram lived until he was twelve years old. Here his brother Elnathan, who became a surgeon in the United States Navy, was born May 28, 1794. Here too, when Adoniram was eight years old, his sister Mary was born, only to die six months later. This first contact with death must have marked an epoch in his boyish life.

Adoniram was about seven years old, when, having been duly instructed that the earth is a spherical body and that it revolves around the sun, it became a serious question in his mind whether or not the sun moved at all. He might have settled the point by asking his father or mother; but that would have spoiled all his pleasant speculations, and probably would have been the very last thing to occur to him. His little sister, whom alone he consulted, said the sun did move, for she could see it; but he had learned already in this matter to distrust the evidence of his senses, and he talked so wisely about positive proof, that she was astonished and silenced. Soon after this he was one day missed about midday; and as he had not been seen for several hours, his father became uneasy and went in search of him. He was found in a field, at some distance from the house, stretched on his back, his hat with a circular hole cut in the crown laid over his face, and his swollen eyes almost blinded with the intense light and heat. He only told his father that he was looking at the sun; but he assured his sister that he had solved the problem with regard to the sun's moving, though she never could comprehend the process by which he arrived at the result.

He was noted among his companions for uncommon acuteness in the solution of charades and enigmas, and retained a great store of them in his memory for the purpose of puzzling his schoolfellows. On one occasion he found in a newspaper an enigma rather boastfully set forth, and accompanied by a challenge for a solution. He felt very sure that he had "guessed riddles as hard as that," and gave himself no rest until he had discovered a satisfactory answer. This he copied out in as fair a hand as possible, addressed it to the editor, and confiding in no one but his sister, conveyed it to the post-office. But the postmaster supposed it to be some mischievous prank of the minister's son, and he accordingly placed the letter in the hands of the father. The poor boy's surprise and discomfiture may be imagined when he saw it paraded on the table after tea.

"Is that yours, Adoniram?"

"Yes, sir."

"How came you to write it?"

Silence.

"What is it about?"

Falteringly, "Please read it, father."

"I do not read other people's letters. Break the seal and read it yourself."

Adoniram broke the seal and mumbled over the contents, then placed the letter in his father's hands. He read it, called for the newspaper which had suggested it, and after reading and re-reading both, laid them on the table, crossed his hands on his knees, and looked intently into the fire. Meanwhile Adoniram stood silently watching his countenance, speculating on the chances of his being treated as a culprit, or praised for his acuteness. But the father awoke from his reverie, the subject of conversation was changed, and the letter never heard of afterward. The next morning Adoniram's father gravely informed him that he had purchased for his use a book of riddles, a very common one, but as soon as he had solved all that it contained, he should have more difficult books.

"You are a very acute boy, Adoniram," he added, patting him on the head with unusual affection ; "and I expect you to become a great man."

Adoniram seized upon the book of riddles joyfully, and was a good deal surprised and disappointed to find it the veritable arithmetic which the larger boys in Master Dodge's school were studying. But then his father had praised him, and if there was anything puzzling in the arithmetic, he was sure he should like it ; and so he prepared to enter upon the study with alacrity. Before reaching his tenth year, he had gained quite a reputation for good scholarship, especially in arithmetic.

A gentleman residing in the neighboring town of Beverly sent him a problem, with the offer of a dollar for the solution. Adoniram immediately shut himself in his chamber. The reward was tempting; but more important still, his reputation was at stake. On the morning of the second day he was called from his seclusion to amuse his little brother, who was ill. He went reluctantly, but without murmuring, for the government of his parents was of a nature that no child would think of resisting. His task was to build a cob house. He laid an unusually strong foundation, with unaccountable slowness and hesitation, and was very deliberately proceeding with the superstructure, when suddenly he exclaimed: "That's it! I've got it!" and sending the materials for the half-built house rolling about the room, he hurried off to his chamber to record the result. The problem was solved, the dollar was won, and the boy's reputation established.

At the age of ten he was sent to one Captain Morton, of whom he took lessons in navigation, in which he is said to have made decided progress. In the grammar school he was noted for his proficiency in the Greek language. His schoolmates nicknamed him "Virgil," or in allusion to the peculiar style of the hat which he wore, as well as to his studious habits, "old Virgil dug up." As a boy he was spirited, self-confident, and exceedingly enthusiastic, very active and energetic, but fonder of his books than of play. His sister has a vivid recollection of his affectionate tenderness toward her, and of his great kindness to the inferior animals. He was very fond of desultory reading; and as there were no books for children at that period, he alternated between the books of theology found in his father's library, and the novels of Richardson and Fielding, or the plays of Ben Jonson, which he was able to borrow in the neighborhood. It is not probable that his father encouraged this latter class of reading, but the habits of self-dependence which he had thought proper to cultivate in his son, left his hours of leisure mostly untrammelled; and seeing the greediness with which the boy occasionally devoured books of the gravest character, it very likely had not occurred to him that he could feel the least possible interest in any work of the imagination.

Before Adoniram was twelve years of age, he had

heard visitors at his father's talk a great deal of a new exposition of the Apocalypse, which they pronounced a work
of rare interest. Now the Revelation was the book that,
of all others in the Bible, he delighted most to read, and
he had searched the few commentators his father possessed
without getting much light upon its mysteries. The new
exposition was owned by a very awe-inspiring gentleman
in the neighborhood; but Adoniram felt that he *must*
have it, and after contending a long time with his bash-
fulness, he at last determined on begging the loan of it.
He presented himself in the great man's library, and was
coldly and sternly refused. For once his grief and mor-
tification were so great that he could not conceal the affair
from his father. He received more sympathy than he
anticipated. "Not lend it to you!" said the good man,
indignantly; "I wish *he* could understand it half as
well. You shall have books, Adoniram, just as many as
you can read, and I'll go to Boston myself for them."
He performed his promise, but the desired work on the
Apocalypse, perhaps for judicious reasons, was not obtained.

In the year 1800, the family removed to Braintree,
Mass., and two years later, when Adoniram was fourteen
years old, took up their abode in the old historic town of
Plymouth. In 1804 he entered Rhode Island College—
now Brown University—one year in advance. During his college course he was a hard student; and in
1807, at the age of nineteen, was graduated the valedicto-
rian of his class, in spite of the fact that for six weeks of
the senior year he was absent, engaged in teaching school
in Plymouth. He was ambitious to excel, and a classmate
says of him, he has no recollection of his ever failing, or
even hesitating, in recitation. He had a powerful rival

in his friend Bailey,[1] and this probably added zest to his ambition.   When he received the highest appointment in the commencement exercises, his delight knew no bounds. He hurried to his room, and wrote, "Dear father, I have got it.   Your affectionate son, A. J."   He then took a circuitous route to the post-office, that he might quiet the violent throbbing of his heart, and appear with propriety before his classmates, and especially before his rival friend.

In the autumn of 1807, young Judson opened in Plymouth a private academy, which he taught for nearly a year.   During this time he also published two text-books, "The Elements of English Grammar," and "The Young Lady's Arithmetic."   But the most important event of this period of his life was his conversion.

When about fourteen years of age, his studies were interrupted by a serious illness, by which he was reduced to a state of extreme weakness, and for a long time his recovery was doubtful.   It was more than a year before he was able to resume his customary occupations. Previous to this he had been too actively engaged to devote much time to thought; but as soon as the violence of the disease subsided, he spent many long days and nights in reflecting on his future course.   His plans were of the most extravagantly ambitious character.   Now he was an orator, now a poet, now a statesman; but whatever his character or profession, he was sure in his castle-building to attain the highest eminence.   After a time, one thought crept into his mind and embittered all his musings.   Suppose he should attain the very highest pinnacle of which human nature is capable; what then? Could he hold his honors forever?   His favorites of other ages had long since turned to dust, and what

---

[1] The late Hon. John Bailey, member of Congress from Massachusetts,

was it to them that the world still praised them? What would it be **to** him, when **a** hundred years had gone by, that America had never known his equal? He did not wonder that Alexander wept when at the summit of his ambition; he felt very sure that he should have wept too. Then he would become alarmed at the extent of his own wicked soarings, and try to comfort himself with the idea that it was all the result of the fever in his brain.

One day his mind reverted to religious pursuits. Yes, an eminent divine was very well, though he should of course prefer something more brilliant. Gradually, and without his being aware of his own train of thought, his mind instituted a comparison between the great worldly divine, toiling for the same perishable objects as his other favorites, **and** the humble minister of the gospel, laboring only to please God and benefit his fellow-men. There **was** (so he thought) a sort of sublimity about that, after **all.** Surely the world was all wrong, or such a self-abjuring man would be its hero. Ah, but the good man had a reputation more enduring! Yes, yes, his fame **was** sounded before him as he entered the other world; and that was the only fame worthy of the possession, because the only one that triumphed over the grave. Suddenly, in the midst of his self-gratulation, the words flashed across his mind, "Not unto us, not unto us, but to Thy name be the glory." He **was** confounded. Not that he had actually made himself the representative of this last kind of greatness—it was not **sufficiently** to his taste for that; but he had ventured on dangerous ground, and he **was** startled by a flood of feelings that had till now remained dormant. He had always said **and** thought, so far as he had thought anything about it, that he wished to become **truly** religious; but **now** religion seemed so entirely op

posed to all his ambitious plans that he was afraid to
look into his heart lest he should discover what he did
not like to confess, even to himself—that he did not want
to become a Christian. He was fully awake to the vanity
of worldly pursuits, and was, on the whole, prepared to
yield the palm of excellence to religious ones; but his
father had often said he would one day be a great man,
and a great man he had resolved to be.

It was at this period that French infidelity was sweeping over the land like a flood, and free inquiry in
matters of religion was supposed to constitute part of the
education of every man of spirit. Young Judson did not
escape the contamination. In the class above him was a
young man by the name of E—— who was amiable,
talented, witty, exceedingly agreeable in person and
manners, but who was a confirmed deist. A very strong
friendship sprang up between the two young men,
founded on similar tastes and sympathies, and Judson
soon became, at least professedly, as great an unbeliever
as his friend. The subject of a profession was often discussed between them. At one time they proposed entering the law, because it afforded so wide a scope for
political ambition; and at another they discussed their
own dramatic powers, with a view to writing plays.

Immediately on closing the school at Plymouth, Judson
set out on a tour through the Northern States. After
visiting some of the New England States, he left the
horse with which his father had furnished him with an
uncle in Sheffield, Conn., and proceeded to Albany to see
the wonder of the world, the newly invented Robert
Fulton steamer. She was about proceeding on her second
trip to New York, and he gladly took passage in her.
The magnificent scenery of the Hudson had then excited

comparatively little attention, and its novelty and sublimity could not fail to make a deep and lasting impression on one of Judson's ardent and adventurous spirit.
Indeed, during his last illness, he described it with all the
enthusiasm that might have characterized his youth. His
name was frequently mistaken for that of Johnson; and
it occurred to him that, in the novel scenes before him,
he might as well use this convenient disguise, in order to
see as deeply into the world as possible. He therefore,
without actually giving out the name with distinctness
or ever writing it down, became Mr. Johnson. He had
not been long in New York before he contrived to attach
himself to a theatrical company, not with the design of
entering upon the stage, but partly for the purpose of
familiarizing himself with its regulations in case he
should enter upon his literary projects, and partly from
curiosity and love of adventure.

Before setting out upon his tour he had unfolded his
infidel sentiments to his father, and had been treated with
the severity natural to a masculine mind that has never
doubted, and to a parent who, after having made innum-
erable sacrifices for the son of his pride and love, sees
him rush recklessly on to his own destruction. His
mother was none the less distressed, and she wept, and
prayed, and expostulated. He knew his superiority to
his father in argument; but he had nothing to oppose to
his mother's tears and warnings, and they followed him
now wherever he went. He knew that he was on the
verge of a life he despised. On no consideration would
he see a young brother in his position; but "I," he
thought, "am in no danger—I am only seeing the world
—the dark side of it, as well as the bright; and I have
too much self-respect to do anything mean or vicious."

After seeing what he wished of New York, he returned
to Sheffield for his horse, intending to pursue his journey
westward.   His uncle, Rev. Ephraim Judson, was absent,
and a very pious young man occupied his place.   His
conversation was characterized by a godly sincerity, a
solemn but gentle earnestness which addressed itself to
the heart, and Judson went away deeply impressed.

The next night he stopped at a country inn.   The
landlord mentioned, as he lighted him to his room, that
he had been obliged to place him next door to a young
man who was exceedingly ill, probably in a dying state;
but he hoped that it would occasion him no uneasiness.
Judson assured him that, beyond pity for the poor sick
man, he should have no feeling whatever, and that now,
having heard of the circumstance, his pity would not of
course be increased by the nearness of the object.   But it
was nevertheless a very restless night.   Sounds came
from the sick chamber—sometimes the movements of the
watchers, sometimes the groans of the sufferer; but it
was not these which disturbed him.   He thought of what
the landlord had said—the stranger was probably in a
dying state; and was he prepared?   Alone, and in the
dead of night, he felt a flush of shame steal over him at
the question, for it proved the shallowness of his philosophy.   What would his late companions say to his
weakness?   The clear-minded, intellectual, witty E——,
what would he say to such consummate boyishness?   But
still his thoughts *would* revert to the sick man.   Was he
a Christian, calm and strong in the hope of a glorious
immortality, or was he shuddering upon the brink of a
dark, unknown future?   Perhaps he was a "freethinker,"
educated by Christian parents, and prayed over by a
Christian mother.   The landlord had described him as a

young man; and in imagination he was forced to place himself upon the dying bed, though he strove with all his might against it. At last morning came, and the bright flood of light which it poured ˉinto his chamber dispelled all his "superstitious illusions." As soon as he had risen, he went in search of the landlord, and inquired for his fellow-lodger.

" He is dead," was the reply.

" Dead! "

" Yes; he is gone—poor fellow! The doctor said he would probably not survive the night."

" Do you know who he was? "

" Oh, yes; it was a young man from Rhode Island College—a very fine fellow; his name was E——." Judson was completely stunned. After hours had passed, he knew not how, he attempted to pursue his journey. But one single thought occupied his mind, and the words, dead! lost! lost! were continually ringing in his ears. He knew the religion of the Bible to be true; he felt its truth; and he was in despair. In this state of mind he resolved to abandon his scheme of traveling, and at once turned his horse's head toward Plymouth.

He arrived at Plymouth, September 22, 1808, and in October of the same year entered the Theological Institution at Andover, one year in advance. As he was neither a professor of religion nor a candidate for the ministry, he was admitted only by special favor. On the 2d of December, 1808, he made a solemn dedication of himself to God, and on the 28th of May, 1809, at the age of twenty-one, he joined the Third Congregational Church in Plymouth. His conversion involved in itself a consecration to the Christian ministry.

CHAPTER II

IN September, 1809, young Judson, at the age of twenty-one, began to ponder seriously the subject of foreign missions. He had just finished his first year of study at Andover; another year of the theological course remained. At this time there fell into his hands a sermon preached in the parish church of Bristol, England, by Dr. Claudius Buchanan, who had for many years been a chaplain in the service of the British East India Company. The sermon was entitled, "The Star in the East," and had for its text Matt. 2 : 2 : "For we have seen his star in the east, and are come to worship him." The leading thought of the sermon was the evidences of the divine power of the Christian religion in the East. Dr. Buchanan described the progress of the gospel in India, and especially the labors of the venerable German missionary, Schwartz. This sermon fell like a spark into the tinder of Judson's soul.

Six months from the time of his reading this sermon, he made the final resolve to become a missionary to the heathen. This was in February, 1810. He was, no doubt, stimulated to form this purpose by close contact with several other young men of like aspirations. His earliest missionary associate was Samuel Nott, Jr., who entered the seminary early in the year 1810, and was even then weighing the question whether he should devote himself to the work of carrying the gospel to the heathen.

22

THE HAYSTACK MONUMENT AT WILLIAMSTOWN, MASS.

Adoniram Judson.   Page 23.

About the same time there came to Andover four young men from Williams College—Samuel J. Mills, Jr., James Richards, Luther Rice, and Gordon Hall. While in college these students formed a missionary society, and they were accustomed to meet together at night beneath a haystack near the college grounds. At Williamstown, on the spot where now stands the famous Haystack Monument, these young men consecrated themselves to the work of foreign missions, and poured out their fervent prayers for the conversion of the world; and this green nook among the Berkshire hills may well be called the birthplace of American foreign missions.

As great scientific discoveries have seemed to spring up almost simultaneously in the minds of independent and widely separated thinkers, sometimes engendering a strife as to the original discoverer, so this grand thought of evangelizing the heathen seems to have been in the atmosphere, and to have floated at almost the same time into the hearts of different young men living far apart. Christian society was like a field which, having been ploughed and sown, has folded up in its bosom a potency of growth. Judson and his associates were like the first green shoots, scattered far and wide, that appear above the ground and promise to be followed by countless others. It was after long meditation and prayer, and in communion with kindred glowing spirits, that the thought in Judson's mind of consecrating himself to the foreign missionary work became a fixed purpose.

There were many obstacles in the way. He was not going among the heathen because he could not find suitable employment at home. He had received a tutor's appointment in Brown University and had declined it. The Rev. Dr. Griffin had proposed him as his colleague in "the largest church in Boston." "And you will be so near home," his mother said. "No!" was his reply. "I shall never live in Boston. I have much farther than that to go." The ambitious hopes of his father were overthrown; and his mother and sister shed many regretful tears. He did not go abroad because he was not wanted at home.

But what steps did he and his young associates take in order to execute their sublime purpose? There was at that time no foreign missionary society in America to which they could offer their services, and which would undertake their support in the foreign field. There was, indeed, the Massachusetts Missionary Society, founded in 1799, the object of which was to diffuse a missionary spirit among the Congregational churches in New England, and to carry the gospel to the Indians and to the newly settled parts of our own land. But this society had not yet launched upon the work of foreign missions; and so Mr. Judson and the young men who shared his purpose first proposed to each other to enlist as missionaries under the London Missionary Society. Accordingly Mr. Judson wrote a letter to that effect to the venerable Dr. Bogue, the president of the seminary in Gosport, England, where the missionaries of the London society received their training.

While awaiting a reply to this letter, he and his associates made their desires known to their teachers in the seminary, and to several influential ministers in the vicinity. The professors and ministers met for consultation on the matter at the house of Prof. Stuart, in Andover, on Monday, June 25, 1810. These wise and conservative men advised the students to submit their case to the General Association, a body representing all the Congregational churches of the State of Massachusetts, and which was to meet at Bradford the next day.

Thus the action of these students led to the organization of the American Board of Commissioners for Foreign Missions, a society widely known and justly revered at the present day as the missionary organ of the Congregational church of America, and indeed the mother of American foreign missionary societies.

The nine men originally forming this Board distrusted their ability to support in the foreign field those who had offered their services. They feared that the missionary sentiment among the churches of New England was hardly strong enough as yet to undertake so great an enterprise; and so they turned instinctively to their brethren in England, represented in the London Missionary Society, for aid and co-operation. They accordingly sent Mr. Judson to England to ascertain whether such co-operation would be agreeable to the London society.

The English directors gave Mr. Judson a most courteous and affectionate greeting, but a joint conduct of the missions did not seem practicable to them. They were willing to receive and support Mr. Judson and his associates as their own missionaries, but did not feel disposed to admit the American Board to a participation with them in the direction of the work. Such co-operation might occasion complications, and they wisely thought that American Christians were able to take care of their own missionaries.

Mr. Judson embarked for England, January 11, 1811, on the English ship "Packet." She was captured on the way by a French privateer, and so he was subjected to compulsory detention and imprisonment in France. On the 6th of May he arrived in London, and on the 18th of June he embarked at Gravesend, in the ship "Augustus," bound for New York, where he arrived on the 17th of August.

Soon after Mr. Judson returned to America, on the 18th of September, 1811, the American Board of Commissioners for Foreign Missions met at Worcester, Mass., and advised him and his associates not to place themselves at present under the direction of the London Missionary Society. It was also voted that " Messrs. Adoniram Judson, Jr., Samuel Nott, Jr., Samuel Newell, and Gordon Hall be appointed missionaries to labor under the direction of this Board in Asia, either in the Burman Empire, or in Surat, or in Prince of Wales Island, or elsewhere, as in the view of the Prudential Committee, Providence shall open the most favorable door." Thus the way was prepared for Mr. Judson to realize his ardent desire to become a missionary to the heathen.

But he was not to go alone, for he was already betrothed to Miss Ann Hasseltine. They met for the first time on the memorable occasion already described, when in June, 1810, the General Association held its session at Bradford, and young Judson and his fellow students modestly made known their desires to attempt a mission to the heathen. The story is told that during the sessions the ministers gathered for a dinner beneath Mr. Hasseltine's roof. His youngest daughter, Ann, was waiting on the table. Her attention was attracted to the young student whose bold missionary projects were making such a stir. But what was her surprise to observe, as she moved about the table, that he seemed completely absorbed in his plate! Little did she dream that she had already woven her spell about his young heart, and that he was at that very time composing a graceful stanza in her praise.

She was born in Bradford, December 22, 1789, and was about a year, younger than Mr Judson. Her parents were John and Rebecca Hasseltine. She had an ardent, active, even restless temperament; so that her mother once reproved her in childhood with the ominous words, "I hope, my daughter, you will one day be satisfied with rambling." She was educated at the Bradford Academy, and was a beautiful girl, characterized by great vivacity of spirits and intensely fond of society. In fact, she was so reckless in her gayety, and so far outstripped her young companions in mirth, that they feared she would have but a brief life, and be suddenly cut off. At the age of sixteen she was converted, and threw herself with all her native ardor into the joys and labors of the Christian life. She taught school for several years in Salem, Haverhill, and Newbury. Her constant endeavor was to bring her pupils to the Saviour.

Her decision to become a foreign missionary must have required great heroism, for thus far no woman had ever left America as a missionary to the heathen. Public sentiment was against her going. It was thought to be wild and romantic. One good lady said to another, "I hear that Miss Hasseltine is going to India! Why does she go?" "Why, she thinks it her duty. Wouldn't you go if you thought it your duty?" "But," replied the lady, with emphasis, "I would not think it my duty!"[1]

On the 5th of February, 1812, Mr. Judson and Ann Hasseltine, were married at Bradford. Two days before, at Plymouth, he had taken final leave of his parents, and his brother Elnathan accompanied him to Boston.

---

[1] For further particulars concerning Miss Hasseltine's early life the reader is referred to her biography, by the Rev. J. D. Knowles.

The journey was made on horseback, and at the time
Elnathan had not been converted. While on the way
the two dismounted, and among the trees by the roadside
they knelt, and there Adoniram offered a fervent prayer
in behalf of his younger brother. Four days later they
parted, never to meet again on earth. The wayside
prayer was not unheeded in heaven. Years afterward,
Adoniram was permitted to have the assurance that the
brother over whom his heart so fondly yearned became
an "inheritor of the kingdom of heaven."

On the 6th of February, he received ordination at
Salem from the Rev. Drs. Spring, Worcester, Woods,
Morse, and Griffin; on the 7th he bade good-bye to his
younger sister and companion of his childhood; and on
the 19th embarked at Salem, with Mrs. Judson, and Mr.
and Mrs. Newell, on the brig "Caravan," Captain
Heard, bound for Calcutta.

CHAPTER III

VOYAGE TO BURMA. 1812, 1813

AFTER the shores of America had faded from their eyes, almost four months elapsed before Mr. Judson and his missionary associates caught sight of land. They made the long trip around the Cape of Good Hope, and at last descried the towering mountains of Golconda. Now that the Suez Canal has been opened, and a railroad track laid across our continent, the missionary to India goes either through the Mediterranean Sea, or by the way of San Francisco and Yokohama, and the voyage consumes only about two months.

While taking the long voyage from America to India, Mr. Judson changed his denominational latitude and longitude as well. He was a Congregational minister; his parents were Congregationalists; and he had been sent out by a Congregational Board. All his sympathies and affections were bound up with the life of that great denominational body. On his way to Burma, however, he became a Baptist. His attention was at this time especially drawn to the distinctive views of the Baptists by the fact that he was now about to found a new Christian society among the heathen. When the adult heathen accepted Christ by faith and love he should of course be baptized, and thus formally initiated into the Christian church. But, ought the children also to be baptized upon the strength of the parents' faith? This was a practical question.

29

Again, Mr. Judson expected to meet in India the eminent English Baptist missionaries, Carey, Marshman, and
Ward.   In the immediate neighborhood of these men
he proposed to institute a Congregationalist form of
church life, and he would of course have to explain to
the natives these denominational differences.   His mind
was cast in a scholarly and argumentative mold.   Con-
troversy might possibly arise between himself and the
Baptist missionaries.   He thought it best while he was
on the ocean to arm himself beforehand for the encounter
with these formidable champions, in order successfully to
maintain the Pedobaptist position.

In the enforced seclusion of a long sea voyage he had
plenty of time for thought and study on this important
subject.   The result of his search and investigation was
the conclusion, reluctantly formed, that he was wrong
and that the Baptists were right.   Of course they held
many fundamental doctrines in common with Christians
of all other evangelical denominations; but there were
two distinctive tenets, that faith should always precede
baptism, and that baptism is immersion.   He was convinced that in these views they had the Bible on their
side.

It was only after a great struggle that he yielded; for
he had to break with all the traditions and associations
of his ancestry and childhood.   He pictured to himself
the grief and disappointment of his Christian friends in
America, especially of his venerable parents.   He saw
that he would be separated from those young students,
the choice companions with whom he had originated this
great scheme of American foreign missions.   In their
discussions, his wife always took the Pedobaptist side.
He knew that he and she might find themselves without

bread in a strange, heathen land. For who could expect the American Board to sustain a Baptist missionary, even if he could on his part obey their instructions? He could have little hope that the Baptists of America, feeble, scattered, and despised, would be equal to the great undertaking of supporting an expensive mission in distant India. Ah! what long anxious conversations must he and his wife have had together in their little cabin on the brig "Caravan."

The question may have arisen in his mind, are these doctrines so important after all? Can I not cherish them in secret, and still remain identified with the religious body that I so much love and honor? No; because if individual faith is the prerequisite of baptism, what scriptural authority would we have for baptizing the unconscious infant? If baptism is a symbol, then of course the form is all important. If faith must precede baptism, and if immersion is essential to baptism, then he himself had never been baptized at all. He knew that baptism had been expressly commanded by our blessed Lord, and that alone was sufficient to necessitate obedience. Prompt and straightforward obedience to Christ was the keynote of his life. His was too positive a character to try to effect a compromise between conviction and action. He had one of those great natures that cannot afford to move along with the crowd.

The four missionaries arrived in Calcutta on June 17th, and were warmly welcomed by Dr. Carey. They were invited to visit the settlement of English Baptists at Serampore, a town about twelve miles from Calcutta, up the Hugli River. Here they awaited the arrival of the other group of American missionaries, Mr. and Mrs. Nott and Messrs. Hall and Rice, who had sailed from Philadelphia

in the ship "Harmony," and who did not arrive until
August 8th. On September 6th, Mr. and Mrs. Judson were
baptized in Calcutta by the Rev. Mr. Ward, and on the first
of November, Mr. Rice, one of his missionary associates
who, though sailing on a different vessel, had experienced
a similiar change of sentiment, was also baptized. " Mr.
Rice was thought," Dr. Carey says, " to be the most obstinate Pedobaptist of any of the missionaries."

But becoming Baptists was only the beginning of
trouble for these missionaries. India was ruled by the
East India Company, which was opposed to the intro-
duction of missionaries, especially of Americans—for
England and America were not at that time on friendly
terms. Besides, the English feared that the natives of
India, finding themselves beset by the missionaries of a
foreign religion, and their own sacred institutions undermined, would rise against the whole English race, and a
war ensue which would be rendered more intense by the
spirit of religious fanaticism. The Oriental meekly sub-
mits to oppression, except where religious questions are
involved ; it was the greased cartridge which brought on
the Sepoy rebellion. The English authorities feared, as
once was stated in the House of Lords, " That every
missionary would have to be backed by a gunboat."
There might arise endless complications, and they determined to arrest the danger before it really began.

Mr. and Mrs. Judson and Mr. Rice were peremptorily
ordered to repair from Serampore to Calcutta. When
they appeared at the government house 'they were told
that they must at once return to America. They asked
leave to settle in some other part of India, but this was
refused. They then asked if they could go to the Isle of
France (Mauritius). This request was granted ; but the

only ship then setting sail for that port could convey but two passengers, and by common consent Mr. and Mrs. Newell embarked. Mr. and Mrs. Judson and Mr. Rice remained behind for another vessel. After two months, they received an order to go on board one of the company's vessels bound for England, and their names were even printed in the official list of passengers. But a vessel named the " Creole " was just about to sail for the Isle of France. They applied to the government for a passport. This was refused. Then they asked the captain if he would take them without a passport. He said, good-naturedly, " There was his ship ; they could go on board if they pleased." They immediately embarked under cover of the night. But while sailing down the Hugli River from Calcutta to the sea they were overtaken by a government dispatch. The pilot was forbidden to go farther, as there were persons on board who had been ordered to England. They were put ashore on the bank of a river and took shelter at a little tavern, while the vessel continued her course down the river without them.

After three or four days, however, a letter came from Calcutta containing the much-desired passport to sail on the " Creole." Who procured the passport has always remained a mystery. But now they had every reason to suppose that the vessel had got out to sea. She might, however, be anchored at Sangur, seventy miles below. With all haste they put their baggage in a boat and sped down the river. They had to row against the tide, but arrived at Sangur before the evening of the next day, and had the happiness of finding the vessel at anchor. " I never enjoyed," says Mrs. Judson, " a sweeter moment in my life than that when I was sure we were in sight

C

of the ' Creole.' '"   After a voyage of six weeks they arrived in Port Louis, on the Isle of France, January 17,
1813.

The Isle of France, or Mauritius, lies in the Indian
Ocean, four hundred and eighty miles east of Madagas-
car.   It is about thirty-six miles long and thirty-two
wide.   It had only a few years before been wrested from
the French by the English.   During the wars between
the French and the English it had furnished harborage
for the French privateers which, sallying forth from its
ports, attacked the richly freighted English merchantmen
on their way from England.   The scene of St. Pierre's
pathetic tale of "Paul and Virginia," it was to our missionaries also who took refuge here, a place of sorrow.
They learned of a death which rivals in pathos the fate
of Virginia.   Mrs. Harriet Newell, the first American
martyr to foreign missions, had only just survived the
tempestuous voyage from Calcutta, and had been laid in
the "heathy ground" of Mauritius; one who "for the
love of Christ and immortal souls, left the bosom of her
friends and found an early grave in a land of strangers."
She never repented leaving her native country.   When
informed by her physician of her approaching death, she
lifted up her hands in triumph, and exclaimed, "Oh,
glorious intelligence!"[1]

What a sense of desolation must have crept over the
little band of missionaries, now that death had so early
broken into their ranks!   On February 24th, Mr. Newell
embarked for Ceylon, and on the 15th of March, Mr.
Rice sailed for America in order to preach a missionary
crusade among the Baptist churches there; and thus Mr.

---

[1] For further particulars see "Memoir of Mrs. Harriet Newell," by Dr.
Leonard Woods.

and Mrs. Judson were left alone. They were obliged to remain about four months on the Isle of France; and while much of their time was spent - in self-sacrificing labors among the English soldiers who formed the garrison of the island, the missionaries still longed to reach their final destination. Mrs. Judson writes: "Oh, when will my wanderings terminate? When shall I find some little spot that I can call my own?" Her mother's ominous words, uttered long ago, were coming true. She was indeed having her fill of "rambling." They had left America nearly fifteen months before, and yet after all their journeyings they seemed no nearer a field of labor than when they first set out. Their destination was still a mirage—an ever-dissolving view.

They decided to make another descent upon the coast of India. On May 7, 1813, they embarked on the ship "Countess of Harcourt," for Madras, intending to establish a mission on Pulo Penang, or Prince of Wales Island, lying in the straits of Malacca. It was a little island of commodious harbors and salubrious climate, which had recently been purchased by the English, and the small native population of Malays was being rapidly increased by emigration from Hindustan, Burma, Siam, and China. On June 4th, they arrived in Madras, where they were kindly received by the English missionaries. Mr. and Mrs. Loveless. But they knew that they could not remain long, for they were again under the jurisdiction of the East India Company. Their arrival was at once reported to the governor-general, and they feared they would be immediately transported to England. There was no vessel in the harbor bound for Pulo Penang, and the only vessel about to sail in that direction was bound for Rangoon, Burma. They dreaded to pass

from the protection of the British flag into the power of
the Burman despot, whose tender mercies were cruel.
But their only alternative was between Rangoon and
their native land, and they chose the former.

On June 22d, the went on board the crazy, old vessel
"Georgiana." The captain was the only person on
board who could speak their language, and they had no
other apartment than that made by canvas. The passage
was very tedious. Mrs. Judson was taken dangerously
ill, and continued so until at one period her husband
came to experience the awful sensation which necessarily
resulted from the expectation of an immediate separation
from his beloved wife, the only remaining companion of
his wanderings. About the same time, the captain being
unable to make the Nicobar Island, where it was intended
to take in a cargo of cocoanuts, they were driven into a
dangerous strait, between the Little and Great Andamans,
two savage coasts where the captain had never been, and
where, if they had been cast ashore they would, according
to all accounts, have been killed and eaten by the natives.
But as one evil is sometimes an antidote to another, so it
happened with them. Their being driven into this dangerous but quiet channel brought immediate relief to the
almost exhausted frame of Mrs. Judson, and conduced
essentially to her recovery. And in the event, they were
safely conducted over the black rocks which they sometimes saw in the gulf below, and on the eastern side of
the islands found favorable winds, which gently wafted
them forward to Rangoon. But on arriving there, other
trials awaited them.

They had never before seen a place where European
influence had not contributed to smooth and soften the
rough, native features. The prospect of Rangoon, as

they approached, was quite disheartening. Mr. Judson
went on shore just at night to take a view of the place
and the mission house; but so dark and cheerless and
unpromising did all things appear that the evening of
that day, after his return to the ship, he and his wife
marked as the most gloomy and distressing that they ever
passed.

However, on July 13th, they reached Rangoon, and
took possession of the English Baptist mission house,
occupied by a son of Dr. Carey. This young man was
temporarily absent, and soon afterward resigned the mission in their favor, and entered the service of the Burmese
Government.

When the tidings reached America that Mr. and Mrs.
Judson and Mr. Rice, Congregational missionaries sent
out by the American Board, had been baptized at Calcutta, the Baptists throughout the whole land were filled
with glad surprise. God had suddenly placed at the dis-
posal of the Baptist denomination three fully equipped
missionaries. They were already in the field, and action
must be prompt. Several influential ministers in Massachusetts met at the house of Dr. Baldwin, in Boston, and
organized the "Baptist Society for Propagating the
Gospel in India and other Foreign Parts." They also,
as well as the American Board, first turned instinctively
toward England for counsel and help. They proposed to the Baptist Missionary Society in London that
Mr. Judson should be associated with Messrs. Carey,
Marshman, and Ward, at Serampore; and that the Baptists in England and America should co-operate in the
work of foreign missions. This, however, did not seem
wise to the English brethren, and so America was again
thrown back upon her own resources.

Mr. Rice, upon his return to this country, traveled everywhere, telling the thrilling story of the experiences of these pioneer missionaries. The greatest enthusiasm was aroused, and missionary societies similar to the one in Boston sprang up in the Middle and Southern States. In order to secure concert of action it seemed best that there should be a general convention, in which all these societies might be represented. Accordingly, on the 18th of May, 1814, delegates from Baptist churches and missionary societies throughout the land convened in the First Baptist Church of Philadelphia. These delegates organized a body which was styled, "The General Missionary Convention of the Baptist Denomination in the United States of America for Foreign Missions." The sum of four thousand dollars was put into the treasury, contributed by the local societies, and it was thought an annual income of five thousand two hundred and eighty dollars might be secured. It was the day of small things. In 1845, the Southern brethren withdrew to form a society of their own, called "The Southern Convention." The Northern organization adopted a new constitution, and assumed the name of "The American Baptist Missionary Union." Its receipts for 1893 were over half a million dollars.

Although Mr. Judson's change in denominational attitude occasioned considerable irritation at the time, yet good and wise men of all religious bodies, viewing his conduct from the standpoint of the present, are agreed that it proved a blessing to the Christian world at large. It occasioned the formation of a second missionary society. There came to be two great benevolent forces at work, where there was only one before. What a history-making epoch that was! The action of those consecrated students at Andover led to the formation of The American Board of Commissioners for Foreign Missions and of The American Baptist Missionary Union; the one the organ of the Congregationalists, the other of the Baptists of America. A water-shed was upheaved, from which two beneficent and ever-widening streams flowed forth for the healing of the nations.

Mr. Judson's life also marks the beginning of that wonderful growth which has characterized the Baptist denomination in this country, for in gathering together and rallying for his support the Baptists awoke to self-consciousness. They arrived at the epoch, so momentous in the life either of a society or of an individual, when the infant passes out of a mere sort of vegetable existence into a consciousness of his being and power.

In the history of a social body, as well as of the human infant, the period of self-consciousness is the beginning of all real power. In 1812, the Baptists of America were a scattered and feeble folk, and lacked solidarity. There was little or no denominational spirit. The summons to the foreign field shook them together. A glass of water may be slowly reduced in temperature even to a point one or two degrees below freezing, and yet remain uncongealed, provided it be kept perfectly motionless; if then it is slightly jarred, it will suddenly turn into ice. The Baptist denomination of America was in just such a state of suspense. It needed to be jarred and shaken into solid and enduring form. Mr. Judson's words: "*Should there be formed a Baptist society for the support of a mission in these parts, I should be ready to consider myself their missionary,*" proved to be the crystallizing touch.

CHAPTER IV

BURMA AND BUDDHISM

BURMA is traversed by three parallel rivers that flow southward: the Irawadi, the Sittang, and the Salwen. By far the largest of these is the Irawadi, which is navigable by steamers to Bhamo, eight hundred and forty miles from the mouth. The country is made up of these three parallel river valleys, and the mountain chains which flank them. The land in Asia gradually slopes from the Himalayas southward toward the bay of Bengal. Starting at the south and moving northward, the traveler finds first broad paddy fields, submerged during a part of the year by the network of streams through which the Irawadi finds its way to the sea; then he traverses upland plains; then a rolling country, with ranges of hills; and finally deep forests, high mountains, and the magnificent defiles through which the rivers flow.

The southern part of Burma, like Egypt, owes its fertility to an annual inundation which is thus described by an English officer:[1]

"With the exception of high knolls standing up here and there, and a strip of high ground at the base of the hills, the whole country, fields, roads, bridges, is under water from one to twelve feet or more in depth. Boats are the only means of locomotion for even a few yards. You sail across the country, ploughing through the half-

---

[1] See Forbes' "British Burma."

submerged long grass, piloting a way through the clumps of brushwood and small trees, into the streets of large agricultural villages, where the cattle are seen stabled high up in the houses, twelve feet from the ground; the children are catching fish with lines through the floor; the people are going about their daily concerns, if it is only to borrow a cheroot from their next-door neighbor, in canoes; in short, all the miseries and laughable *contretemps* sometimes pictured in the illustrated papers as caused by floods in Europe, may be seen—with this difference, that every one is so accustomed to them that they never create a thought of surprise."

The northern part of Burma abounds in mountain streams of exquisite beauty. An eyewitness describes them in flowing terms, as follows:[1]

" In some places they are seen leaping in cascades over precipices from fifty to one hundred feet high; in others, spreading out into deep, quiet lakes. In some places they run purling over pebbles of milk-white quartz, or grass-green prase, or yellow jasper, or sky-blue slate, or variegated porphyry; in others, they glide like arrows over rounded masses of granite, or smooth, angular pieces of green stone. In some places nought can be heard but the stunning sounds of 'deep calling unto deep'; in others, the mind is led to musing by the quiet murmur of the brook, that falls on the ear like distant music. The traveler's path often leads him up the middle of one of these streams, and every turn, like that of a kaleidoscope, reveals something new and pleasing to the eye. Here a daisy-like flower nods over the margin, as if to look at her modest face in the reflecting waters; there the lotus-leafed, wild arum stands knee-deep in water, shaking

---

[1] See Mason's " The Natural Productions of Burma."

around with the motion of the stream the dewdrops on
its peltate bosom like drops of glittering quicksilver.
Here the fantastic roots of a willow, sprinkled with its
woolly capsules, come down to the water's edge, or it may
be a eugenia tree, with its fragrant white corymbs, or a
water dillenia, with its brick-red, scaly trunk, and green,
apple-like fruit, occupies its place ; there the long, droop-
ing red tassels of the barringtonia hang far over the
bank, dropping its blossoms on the water, food for numerous members of the carp family congregated below."

The domestic animals of Burma are the ox, buffalo,
horse, and the goat.   The horses are small, and are used
for riding, never as beasts of burden.   The dog is not kept
as a pet or for hunting ; but, as in other Oriental countries, roams about the cities in a half-wild condition,
devouring offal, and at last becomes the victim of famine
and disease.   The jungles swarm with wild animals, the
monkey, elephant, rhinoceros, tiger, leopard, deer, and
wild-cat.   The elephants are caught, tamed, and used for
riding.   The white elephant, or albino, is especially
prized.   A specimen is always kept at court as the in-
signia of royalty, one of the king's titles being, "Lord
of the White Elephant."

Venomous and offensive reptiles and insects abound.
While you are eating your dinner the lizard may drop
from the bamboo rafters upon the table.   As you step
out of your door the gleaming forms of chameleons shoot
up the trunk of your roof-tree and hide themselves in the
branches.   The scorpion, with its painful sting, and the
centipede, with its poisonous bite, may be found in your
garden.   The children must be warned not to race through
the bushes in your compound, lest they encounter the
hated cobra, whose slightest nip is sure and speedy death.

The author remembers his father taking the Burman spear, the only weapon which he ever used, and coming down into the poultry-yard to dispatch a cobra, whose track had been discovered in the dust beneath the house. How much discomfort and suffering are caused even in our own land by rats, mice, snakes, flies, and mosquitoes!. And the foreign missionary has these same pests, but in a more aggravated form. These are larger, more numerous, and in addition to them he has to cope with the white ants, that in armies destroy his furniture, the scorpion, the centipede, the cobra, the tiger.

The inhabitants of Burma belong to the Mongolian race, the characteristics of which are "long, straight hair; almost complete absence of beard; a dark-colored skin varying from a leather-like yellow to a deep brown, or sometimes tending to red; and prominent cheek-bones, generally accompanied by an oblique setting of the eyes." They are described by a modern writer [1] as " of a stout, active, well-proportioned form;. of a brown, but never of an intensely dark complexion, with black, coarse, and abundant hair, and a little more beard than is possessed by the Siamese."

At the time of Mr. and Mrs. Judson's arrival, the population numbered from six to eight millions. This included, however, not only Burmans, who are the ruling race, and dwell mainly in the larger towns and cities, but also several subject races—Shans, Karens, Ka-khy-ens, half-wild people, who live in villages scattered through the jungles and along the mountain streams. These tribes have different habits, and speak a different language from that of the Burmans. They are related to the Burmans somewhat as the North American Indians

---

[1] Major Yule, in his " Embassy to Ava."

are to us, being perhaps the original inhabitants of the country, and having been subjugated at some remote period of the past. It would seem that wave after wave of Mongolian conquerors had swept over the country from the North, and these tribes are the fragments of wrecked races.

Major Yule gives the following graphic description of the mental and moral traits of the Burmese:

"Unlike the generality of the Asiatics, they are not a fawning race. They are cheerful, and singularly alive to the ridiculous; buoyant, elastic, soon recovering from personal or domestic disaster. With little feeling of patriotism they are still attached to their homes, greatly so to their families. Free from prejudices of caste or creed, they readily fraternize with strangers, and at all times frankly yield to the superiority of a European. Though ignorant they are, when no mental exertion is required, inquisitive, and to a certain extent eager for information; indifferent to the shedding of blood on the part of their rulers, yet not individually cruel; temperate, abstemious, and hardy, but idle, with neither fixedness of purpose, nor perseverance. Discipline, or any continued employment, becomes most irksome to them, yet they are not devoid of a certain degree of enterprise. Great dabblers in all mercantile ventures, they may be called (the women especially) a race of hucksters; not treacherous or habitual perverters of the truth, yet credulous and given to monstrous exaggerations; when vested with authority, arrogant and boastful; if unchecked, corrupt, oppressive, and arbitrary; distinguished for bravery, whilst their chiefs are notorious for cowardice; indifferent shots, and though living in a country abounding in forest, not bold followers of field sports."

The soil of Burma is richly productive of all that is needed for food, or clothing, or shelter, or ornament. The chief crops are rice, maize (or Indian corn), wheat, tobacco, cotton, and indigo. It is computed that eighty per cent. of all the rice brought from the East to Europe is produced in the rich 'paddy-fields of British Burma. There is an abundance of delicious fruits—the jack-fruit, the bread fruit, oranges, bananas, guavas, pine-apples, and the cocoanut. After the annual inundation, the subsiding rivers leave behind them in the depression of the ground ponds well stocked with fish. Beef and mutton the Burman learns to forego, as his religion does not allow him to eat cattle or sheep unless they die a natural death. His meal of rice and curry is sometimes enriched by the addition of poultry. The bamboo yields building material for his houses, and the teak forest timber for his ships. The mineral resources are large. The earth yields iron, tin, silver, gold, sapphires, emeralds, rubies, amber, sulphur, arsenic, antimony, coal (both anthracite and bituminous), and petroleum, which is used by all classes in little clay lamps.

Yet at the time of the arrival of our missionaries there was no commerce on a large scale. This is shown by the high rate of interest, twenty-five per cent.; and sixty per cent., when no security was given. The very productiveness of his country made the Burman of fifty years ago feel independent of foreign nations. He took the narrow view that exportation only tended to impoverishment. The government rigidly prohibited all important exportation except that of the cheap and abundant teak timber. Gold and silver and precious stones must not be carried out for fear of reducing the country to poverty. If in those days an English merchant had

carried a large quantity of silks and calicoes to the royal
city, and had exchanged them for five thousand dollars
in gold, he could possess and enjoy the money there, but
he could not, except by bribery, succeed in carrying it
home. His wealth made him practically an exile and a
prisoner. The marble could not be exported, because it
was consecrated to the building of idols and pagodas.
The cotton and the rice could not be exported, lest there
should not be enough left for the clothing and food of
the population. The only commerce worth mentioning
was with China. The Chinese caravans brought overland
large quantities of silk, and received cotton in exchange.

On account of the low state of commerce, the science
of navigation was quite unknown to the Burmans.
When sailors made their little trips in the dry season
along the shores of the bay of Bengal, they took pains
never to pass out of sight of land.

There were no extensive manufactures in Burma, for
these required an accumulation of large capital; and a
man could never be sure that his wealth would not be
wrested from him by the government. And so the chief
article of manufacture was lacquer ware, as this requires
but little capital. Woven strips of bamboo were smeared
with mud, and baked, polished, and varnished, were then
manufactured into beautiful boxes and trays.

Most of the Burmans, however, are engaged in agricultural pursuits. They raise rice and catch fish, which
they pound up into a mass with coarse salt, and so pro-
duce their favorite relish, *ngapee*. Immense quantities
of rice and *ngapee* are carried up the Irawadi in boats,
and are sold at the capital and in the upper provinces
of Burma.

The *government* of Independent Burma was an absolute despotism, now wholly set aside by the English conquest. The king had supreme power over the life and possessions of every subject. He could confiscate property, imprison, torture, or execute at his pleasure—his only restraint being fear of an insurrection. An English writer relates that at the sovereign's command one of the highest officers of the State was seized by the public executioner and stretched on the ground by the side of the road under a scorching sun, with a heavy weight upon his chest, and afterward restored to his high position. There were indeed two councils of State, by which the government was administered, but the members of these councils were appointed by the king, and could be degraded or executed at his word. The father of the last monarch of Burma saw the evils of this despotic system, and, in arranging for the succession, formed a plan by which his successor should be subject to limitation by his prime ministers. But the new king, Thebaw, a brutal and licentious boy of twenty, frustrated this benignant purpose. He murdered his counsellors, massacred his blood relations, and Burma that had roused herself for a moment from her long nightmare of despotism sank again into sleep.

The whole country was divided into provinces, townships, districts, and villages. Over each province was a governor, or as the Burmese call him, an *Eater*. Through his underlings he taxed every family. His officers received a share of what they could extort, and the rest was divided with the king. In this way the whole land was a scene of enormous extortion. There were no fixed salaries for government functionaries. The higher officer *ate* a certain province or district. The lower lived on fees and perquisites. Courts of law were cor-

rupted by bribery. It was customary to torture wit-
nesses. The criminal was usually executed by decapi-
tation. He might, however, be disembowelled, or thrown
to wild beasts, or crucified, or have his limbs broken with
a bludgeon—if he could not effect his escape by the
plentiful use of money. Who can estimate the miseries
which the peasantry must have suffered under such a system of bribery and extortion? It is not strange that one
of the Burman monarchs, when he came to the throne,
uttered the exclamation, "Great God, I might as well be
king over a desert!"

The *religion* of Burma is Buddhism. Here, and in
the island of Ceylon, this cult exists in its purest form.
Buddhism as is known originated in India about five hundred years before Christ. Here it succeeded in supplant-
ing the ancient religion of the Hindus, derived from the
Vedas, and called Brahminism.

India was in former times saturated with Brahminical
philosophy and Brahminical ceremonial. The people
were completely priest-ridden. Buddhism was an out-
growth from Brahminism, or perhaps rather a recoil
from it. It was related to it somewhat as Christianity is
to Judaism, or Protestantism to the Romish Church.
For one hundred and fifty years Buddhism had a very
rapid and vigorous growth in India, but soon after the
beginning of the Christian era it began to decay, and in
the eighth and ninth centuries A. D., in consequence of
a great persecution, Buddhism was completely extirpated
in India. The ancient religion, Brahminism, was rein-
stated, and Gautama has comparatively few worshipers
in the land of his birth. But a prophet is not without
honor save in his own country. Buddhism is pervaded
by a missionary spirit, and has won its way by peaceful

persuasion into Ceylon, Burma, Siam, Thibet, and China. It is at the present day the religion of more than four hundred millions of human beings—about one-third of the population of the globe.

Buddhism, like Brahminism, holds the doctrine of transmigration of souls. · The soul is at first united with the lowest forms of organic life. By successive births it may climb into the bodies of spiders, snakes, chameleons, and after long ages may reach the human tenement. Then comes the period of probation. According to its behavior in the flesh it either rises still higher to occupy the glorious forms of demigods and gods, or it relapses little by little into its lowest state, and again takes up its wretched abode in the degraded forms of the lower animals.

> Life runs its rounds of living, climbing up
> From mote and gnat and worm, reptile and fish,
> Bird and shagged beast, man, demon, deva, God,
> To clod and mote again.[1]

" He who is now the most degraded of the demons may one day rule the highest of the heavens ; he who is at present seated on the most honorable of the celestial thrones, may one day writhe amidst all the agonies of a place of torment ; and the worm that we crush under our feet may in the course of ages become a supreme Buddha." [2]

> Eternal process moving on,
>   From state to state the spirit walks,
>   And these are but the shattered stalks
> And ruined chrysalis of one.[3]

---

[1] " The Light of Asia," by Edwin Arnold.
[2] Hardwick's " Christ and other Masters."
[3] Tennyson's " In Memoriam."

This belief pervades the every-day thinking of the most ignorant Burmese. An English officer writes, that "just before the drop fell with a wretched murderer, he himself heard him mutter as his last word, 'May my next existence be a man's, and a long one!'" An old woman, whose grown-up son had died, thought that she recognized that son's voice in the bleating of a neighbor's calf. She threw her arms about the animal, and purchasing it, cherished it until its death as the living embodiment of her own child.

Faith in transmigration accounts for the pious Buddhist's treatment of the lower animals. The priests strain the gnats out of the water they drink. "They do not eat after noon, nor drink after dark, for fear of swallowing minute insects, and they carry a brush on all occasions, with which they carefully sweep every place before they sit down, lest they should inadvertently crush any living creature." Mr. Huxley tells us that a Hindu's peace of mind was completely destroyed by a microscopist who showed him the animals in a drop of water. The Buddhists often build hospitals for sick brutes. Perhaps this deep-seated and hereditary faith in transmigration may account for the singular apathy of the natives to the destruction of life caused by snakes and tigers. In fact, one of their legends represents the founder of their religion as sacrificing his life-blood to slake the parched thirst of a starving tigress.

Although Brahminism and Buddhism both agree in teaching transmigration, they differ widely in their views of God and of the soul. Brahminism is pantheistic; Buddhism atheistic. According to Brahminism, matter has no real existence. All physical forms are the merest illusions. The only real existences are souls. These are all parts of a great divine soul from which they emanate and into which they will at last be reabsorbed, as when a flask of water is broken in the ocean. Buddhism denies the existence not only of matter, but of the soul and of God. It is a system of universal negation. There is no trace in it of a supreme being. All is mere seeming. Nothing is real in past, present, or future.

Again, Brahminism betrays a deep consciousness of sin. It teaches the necessity of doing painful penance and of offering animal sacrifices. Buddhism regards sin as cosmical. There is no such thing as blame or guilt. There is no mediation or pardon. The Buddhist brings no animal to the altar. His worship consists in offering up prayers, and perfumes, and flowers, in memory of the founder of his religion.

Again, Brahminism is aristocratic; Buddhism democratic. Brahminism is the religion of caste. It divides the nation into four classes: the priest, the warrior, the tradesman, and the serf. Besides these, but lowest of all, are pariahs, or *outcastes*—the offspring of intercourse that violated the law of caste. There can be no social mingling of the castes. The condition of the serfs is most wretched and humiliating. The laws of Manu ordain that their abode must be outside the towns, their property must be restricted to dogs and asses, their clothes should be those left by the dead, their ornaments rusty iron; they must roam from place to place; no respectable person must hold intercourse with them; they are to aid as public executioners, retaining the clothes of the dead.

Now Buddhism rejected the system of caste. Gautama taught: "The priest is born of a woman; so is the *outcaste*. My law is a law of grace for all. My doctrine is like the sky. There is room for all without exception, men, women, boys, girls, poor, and rich." The two beautiful stories that follow remind us of the spirit and behavior of our own blessed Lord.

Amanda, an eminent disciple of Gautama, meets an *outcaste* girl drawing water at a well. He asks for a draught. She hesitates, fearing she may contaminate him by her touch. He says, " My sister, I do not ask what is thy caste, or thy descent; I beg for water; if thou canst, give it me." Also, a poor man filled Gautama's alms-bowl with a handful of flowers, while ten thousand bushels of rice from the rich failed.

The founder of Buddhism is called Gautama Siddartha, or Buddha. Gautama was the name of his family, Siddartha his own individual name, and Buddha, "the enlightened one," the surname he acquired by his wisdom. He was born about the year 500 B. C., at Kapilavastu, a few days' journey from Benares, near the base of the Himalayas. His father was an Indian prince, and ruled over a tribe called the Sakyas. Buddha is described as of a gentle, ardent, pensive, philanthropic nature. He was reared in the lap of Oriental luxury, but his earnest nature became weary with pleasure. Intimations of the wretchedness of the peasantry of India penetrated even the palace walls. The winds sweeping over the Æolian harp whispered the miseries of mankind.

> We are the voices of the wandering wind,
> Which moan for rest, and rest can never find;
> Lo! as the wind is, so is mortal life,
> A moan, a sigh, a sob, a storm, a strife.
>
> O Maya's son! because we roam the earth,
> Moan we upon these strings; we make no mirth
> So many woes we see in many lands,
> So many streaming eyes, and wringing hands.[1]

---

[1] "The Light of Asia."

The desire to be a saviour takes possession of his breast. Four ominous sights contribute to fix his pur-pose. He sees in his pleasure grounds an old man, broken and decrepit; again, he meets a man smitten with a malignant disease; again, his eye rests upon a corpse. He learns that such are the destinies of himself and of all his fellow-beings. At last he sees a mendicant monk passing by with his alms-bowl. The young prince resolves to leave his father, his wealth, his power, his wife, his child, and become a homeless wanderer, that he may search out the way of salvation for himself and his fellow-men. He first becomes a Brahminical ascetic, and gives himself over to the severest penance and self-torture. Afterward he abandons this altogether, and at last, while in profoundest meditation under the bo-tree, discovers the way of life. He spends his remaining days in traveling through India preaching his gospel, and gain-ing many disciples. He lives to be an old man, and at last dies with the words on his lips : " Nothing is durable ! "

But one eagerly inquires, What was the *way of salva-tion* that Buddha discovered under the bo-tree, and spent half a century of his life in preaching? Observe suc-cessively the *point of departure,* the *goal,* and the *way.*

Buddha starts out with the idea that misery is the indispensable accompaniment of existence—sorrow is shadow to life. The foundation of his philosophy rests in the densest pessimism. While we are bound up in this material world, we are a prey to disappointment, disease, old age, death. We find ourselves " caught in the com-mon net of death and woe, and life which binds to both." There is no way out of the vast and monotonous cycle of transmigration except into *Nirvana*—the *blowing out*—that is, total extinction.

The highest goal therefore, to which we can attain is
utter annihilation.   That this is the meaning of *Nirvana*
or *Nigban,* seems established beyond a doubt.   The most
eminent authorities on Buddhism, Barthelemy St. Hilaire,
Bigandet, Eugene Burnoul, Spence Hardy, and Max
Müller, all agree with the view presented by Mr. Judson
many years ago, that *Nirvana* or *Nigban* is nothing less
than a total extinction of soul and body.   It is the final
blowing out of the soul, as of a lamp; not its absorption,
as when a "dewdrop slips into the shining sea."   It is

> To perish rather, swallowed up and lost
> In the wide womb of uncreated night,
> Devoid of sense and motion.

But in what *way* is this bliss of annihilation to be
reached?   Only by a long and arduous struggle.   There
are four truths to be believed.   1. There is nothing in
life but sorrow.   2. The root of sorrow is desire.   3.
Desire must be destroyed.   4. The way to destroy desire
is to follow the eightfold path, viz., 1. Right doctrine.
2. Right purpose.   3. Right discourse.   4. Right behavior.   5. Right purity.   6. Right thought.   7. Right
solitude.   8. Right rapture.

But in order to do these eight right things, five commandments must be kept.   1. Not to kill.   2. Not to steal.
3. Not to commit adultery.   4. Not to lie.   5. Not to get in-
toxicated.   And upon these commandments Gautama
himself gives the following commentary:

"He who kills as much as a louse or a bug; he who
takes so much as a thread that belongs to another; he
who with a wishful thought looks at another man's wife;
he who makes a jest of what concerns the advantage of
another; he who puts on his tongue as much as a drop
of intoxicating liquor, has broken the commandments."

There **are** four stages to be arrived at in the way of salvation. 1. The believer has a change of heart, and conquers lust, pride, and anger. 2. He is set free from ignorance, doubt, and wrong belief. 3. He enters the state of universal kindliness. 4. He reaches *Nirvana.*

In this succession of stages Buddha makes right conduct a precedent condition to spiritual knowledge; and so is in striking harmony with a greater than he : " If any man willeth to do his will, he shall know of the doctrine."

It is clear that the strength of Buddhism lies not in its philosophy or theology, but in its code of morals. To its system of rightness rigidly practised by its founder it owes its vitality. If the presentation of a system of morality could save, then long since India, Burma, Ceylon, Siam, Thibet, and China ought to have become an earthly paradise. Besides the virtues ordinarily recognized in heathen codes, Buddhism teaches meekness and forbearance. The pious Buddhist, when struck a violent blow, can meekly reflect that it is in consequence of some sin that he has committed in a previous state of existence. This is a system that teaches us to love our fellow-men tenderly and perseveringly. " As even at the risk of her own life a mother watches over her own child, her only child, so let him—the Buddhist saint—exert good will without measure towards all beings."

But after all, Buddhism, with its exquisite code of morals, has never succeeded in cleansing the Augean stable of the human heart. It is a religion without God, or prayer, or pardon, or heaven. Its laws lack the authority of a law giver. Its *Nirvana* is a cheerless and uninviting prospect. It is a system of despair. The spirits are weighed down by the vast load of demerits and haunted by the anticipation of endless ages of misery. There is no "pity sitting in the clouds." There is no way of forgiveness, no sense of the divine presence and sympathy. Under such a system of cold abstractions, it is not strange that the common people should distort the conception of Nirvana into an earthly paradise, and fly for refuge even into demon worship, and other forms of Shamanism.

In Edwin Arnold's beautiful poem this religion has been presented in a most burnished and fascinating form; but no one whose mind is not filled with misconceptions of Christianity would think for a moment of exchanging the "Light of the World" for the "Light of Asia."

CHAPTER V

MR. AND MRS. JUDSON, as has already been stated, arrived in Rangoon, June 13, 1813. For almost a year and a half after leaving their native land, they had been seeking a home on heathen shores. Having reached Calcutta, they had been forced by the oppressive policy of the East India Company to take refuge upon the Isle of France. They returned again to India and landed at Madras. But they were compelled to flee a second time, and having reluctantly relinquished the strong protection of the British flag, had at last settled down in Rangoon, the chief seaport of the Burman empire. Their own desires and hopes had pointed elsewhere; and it was "with wandering steps and slow" that they had come to this destination. God had drawn around them the relentless toils of his providence, and had hemmed them into this one opening. But subsequent history has proved that the hand which led them so strangely and sternly, was the hand that never errs. American Christians, in their assault upon Asiatic heathenism, could never have chosen a more strategic position than Rangoon. It is situated near the mouth of the great Irawadi River, which is thus described by an English officer:

"After draining the great plain of upper Burma, it enters a narrow valley lying between the spurs of the Arracan and Pegu ranges, and extending below the city

57

of Prome. Thus the mighty stream rolls on through the
widening bay, until about ninety miles from the sea, it
bifurcates; one branch flows to the westward and forms
the Bassein River, while the main channel of the lower
part of the Delta subdivides and finally enters the sea by
ten mouths. It is navigable for river steamers for eight
hundred and forty miles from the sea, but it is during the
rainy season (Monsoon) that it is seen in its full grandeur.
The stream then rises forty feet above its summer level,
and flooding the banks presents in some places, as far as
the eye can reach, a boundless expanse of turbid waters,
the main channel of which rushes along with a velocity
of five miles an hour."

The two natural outlets for the commerce of Western
China are this great river, and the Yang-tse-kiang, which
takes its rise in Thibet, and following an easterly course
of nearly three thousand miles, empties itself into the
Yellow Sea. Along this channel a vast tide of commerce
has followed from time immemorial, and placing upon
the river banks its rich deposits of wealth and population,
has occasioned the growth of Shanghai, Nanking, and
other enormous cities. But the merchandise of Western
and Central China would find a shorter and easier and
cheaper path to the sea through the valley of the
Irawadi, and would long ago have pursued that course,
had it not been impeded and endangered by rude
mountain tribes which the governments of Burma and of
China have not as yet been vigorous enough to reduce to
harmlessness. As civilization advances, a much larger
part of the trade of Central Asia will be sure to find its
way to the sea through the valley of the Irawadi.
Christianity always enters the heart of a nation along the
lines of trade; so that Rangoon, near the mouth of the

Irawadi, where Mr. and Mrs. Judson landed, and Bhamo, situated at the head of navigation, eight hundred and forty miles up the river, where the American Baptists have planted a mission, are two of the most important strategical points for the conquest of all Asia.

Rangoon is described by an American traveler who passed through it about the time of the arrival of the Judsons as: "A miserable, dirty town, containing eight thousand or ten thousand inhabitants, the houses being built with bamboo and teak planks, with thatched roofs—almost without drainage, and intersected by muddy creeks, through which the tide flowed at high water. It had altogether a mean, uninviting appearance, but it was the city of government of an extensive province ruled over by a viceroy, a *woongee* of the empire, in high favor at the court."

It may be well to consider for a moment the *task* which the young missionary had set before him in landing in this heathen land. What did they propose to do, this man of twenty-five and his young wife, standing amid the level rice fields on the coast of Lower Burma, with their faces turned landward toward towns and cities swarming with idolaters, the hill-tops crowned with heathen temples and pagodas? Their purpose was to undermine an ancient religion, deeply fixed in the hearts and habits of four hundred millions of human beings. They did not propose to bring to bear influences by which Christianity was to be introduced as a State religion and reluctant knees be forced to bow to the Christ. This would have been indeed an audacious undertaking. But they sought to work out a more searching revolution, nothing less than a change of belief and of heart in each individual. The millions of Burma were to be taken one by one—

their affections subdued, and their characters transfigured by the religion of Christ. They felt sure that in the mass of people about them there was here and there a man who had been so schooled by the providences of God, and so matured by the Divine Spirit, that if the story of the cross could once be gotten to him he would immediately accept it and say, "That is just what I want." As the sod of moss, brought from the woods into the house, often contains within its bosom hidden germs, and after a season in the warmth of the parlor sends forth sweet, unexpected spring flowers, so out of the unattractive sod of heathenism, under the genial rays of the Holy Spirit, might emerge disciples of Christ, and these disciples, organized by baptism into churches, would, by the same process of reaching individual souls, little by little leaven the whole of the empire.

But what *means* did Mr. Judson use in his endeavor to bring about this great moral and spiritual revolution? Simply the gospel of Christ. The sole weapons of his warfare were the old-fashioned truths, the existence of a personal and beneficent God, the fatal sinfulness of man, and salvation by faith in the Son of God, who came to "seek and to save that which was lost." No system of truth could be devised more diametrically opposed to Buddhism, which teaches that there is no God to save, no soul to be saved, and no sin to be saved from. He felt sure that if he could only plant the seeds of Christian truth in the soil of the Burman's heart, then under the mellowing influence of the Holy Spirit they would germinate and bring forth the fruit of meek and pure behavior. As in flushing a drain a large body of pure water is poured through the whole length of it, washing out every impurity, so the gospel of Christ is a cleansing tide, which as it courses through the individual heart, or through human society, sweeps away before it all the stagnant and loathsome accumulations of sin.

Mr. Judson did not believe that Christianity must needs follow in the wake of civilization. He did not propose to spend his time in teaching the arts and sciences of the Western world, in imparting more correct astronomical, geographical, and geological conceptions, in order, little by little, to prepare the mind of the Burman to accept his religious ideas. He had implicit confidence in the promise of his Master, "Lo, I am with you alway." He believed that Christ was with him in the heart of the heathen, unlocking the door from the inside.

Again, he did not say to himself, "It is a hopeless task to attempt the conversion of the hoary heads. I will try to gather the little children together and establish schools, and thus purify the fountains of national life." He had his schools, indeed, but they were quite subordinate to the work of preaching the gospel to the adult mind. He reached the children through the parents, and not the parents through the children. He believed that the grown-up Burmans, rather than their children, should bear the brunt of persecution involved in embracing a new religion. He followed the method of the Acts of the Apostles. A preacher of the gospel, he did not allow himself to shrivel into a mere school teacher or a school-book maker.

There were only two channels through which the truths of the gospel could be conveyed to the conscience of the Burman—the eyes and the ears. The natives were emphatically a reading people. They had their ancient scriptures embodying the teachings of Gautama, and the first question asked of the propagator of a new religion would be, "Where are your sacred books?" So that one way in which Mr. Judson communicated the gospel was by the translation of tracts—either succinct and concrete statements of Christian truth, or portions of the Bible. These were not scattered about like autumn leaves, but were given discriminatingly to individuals, the gift often being accompanied by a solemn injunction to read, followed by a fervent prayer.

But far more important than the work of translating and distributing tracts, catechisms, and portions of the Scripture, was the oral preaching of the gospel. For this Mr. Judson had rare aptitude, and in it he won his most signal triumphs. While engaged in the necessary work of translation, he was always pining for the opportunity of imparting the message of salvation with the living voice. In a letter to Dr. Bolles he says: "I long to see the whole New Testament complete, for I will then be able to devote all my time to preaching the gospel from day to day; and often now the latter appears to be the more pressing duty. May the Spirit of the Lord be poured out!" When eye meets eye, and the mind of an objector is confronted by a living, loving personality, he receives a deeper impression of religious truth than he can ever get even from the leisurely perusal of a printed book. The press can never supplant the pulpit. The truth which, when pressed home by the earnest voice of the speaker carries with it conviction and arouses the conscience and kindles the affections, is often weak and thin when presented on the printed page.

But Mr. Judson's preaching was unlike that of the orator about whom a great throng gathers. After the little chapel, or *zayat*, was built, public worship indeed was held, the audience consisting of perhaps a hundred per-

*sons. But most of the preaching at first was to the individual. It was a process of spiritual buttonholing. A single person would enter into a discussion with the missionary, while a few others would draw near to witness the encounter. It was in these hand-to-hand frays that Mr. Judson often extorted exclamations of admiration from the bystanders, as with his keen logic he hewed his opponent to pieces as Samuel did Agag.

His preaching was concrete. He did not deal in vague abstractions. Truth assumed in his mind statuesque forms. His conversation abounded in images and illustrations; and in this respect he resembled the great Teacher, whom Tennyson thus described:

> For wisdom dealt with mortal powers,
> Where truth in closest words shall fail,
> When truth embodied in a tale
> Shall enter in at lowly doors.

Behind his words when he preached lay the magnet of a great character. He was a man of tender sensibilities and of strong affections. There was no mistaking his motives. He had come a long distance and endured great hardships because he loved the Burmans—because he loved all men. Little by little they found this out; and the power of a preacher is in direct ratio with his capacity for inspiring confidence and affection.

Difficulties, of course, at once presented themselves. The ardent temperament of the young missionary flung itself against the hard barriers of Burman *conservatism*. Oriental slowness to accept a new idea proved a strong obstacle at the outset. Another great difficulty at the beginning was learning the language without grammar, or dictionary, or an English-speaking teacher.

But the chief hindrance to preaching the gospel to the

Burmans was the danger of persecution. Mr. Judson ▸
found himself in the dominions of a monarch upon whose
slightest nod depended the life of each subject. Every
convert knew that in adopting this new religion he was
encountering the risk of confiscation of property, imprisonment, torture, or death in its most shocking form.

But in spite of these great difficulties, and even in the
face of the fact that many of his brethren and sisters in
his own distant native land regarded the undertaking as
hopeless, and looked upon him as an obstinate and chi-
merical fanatic, he never for a moment lost hope. He
felt as sure that Burma would be converted to Christ as
that it existed. He was buoyed up by the same faith
that caused him to answer many years after, when he was
asked whether he thought the prospects bright for the
speedy conversion of the heathen, "As bright as the
promises of God." And in the darkest period of the
history of our missions, he sounded the bugle call which
will inspire the heart of the Christian missionary until
that day when "The kingdoms of this world are become
the kingdoms of our Lord and of his Christ."

"If any ask what success I meet with among the natives, tell them to look at Otaheite, where the missionaries labored nearly twenty years and, not meeting with
the slightest success, began to be neglected by all the
Christian world, and the very name of Otaheite began to
be a shame to the cause of missions; and now the blessing begins to come. Tell them to look at Bengal also,
where Dr. Thomas had been laboring seventeen years
(that is, from 1783 to 1800,) before the first convert,
Krishna, was baptized. When a few converts are once
made, things move on; but it requires a much longer time
than I have been here to make a first impression on a

heathen people. If they ask again, what prospect of ultimate success is there? tell them, as much as that there is an almighty and faithful God, who will perform his promises, and no more. If this does not satisfy them, beg them to let me stay and try it, and to let you come, and to give us our *bread;* or, if they are unwilling to risk their bread on such a forlorn hope as has nothing but the word of God to sustain it, beg of them, at least, not to prevent others from giving us bread; and, if we live some twenty or thirty years, they may hear from us again."

After a few months Mr. and Mrs. Judson removed from the English Baptist mission house into the city proper. The mission house which they had been occupying was situated half a mile from Rangoon, near the place of public execution, where the refuse of the city streets was thrown, and not far from the place where the dead were buried. While outside the city walls, the missionaries were exposed to robbers and to wild beasts. It was thought best, therefore, to move into the city itself, especially as in this way they would be brought into closer contact with the people.

After they had been in Rangoon about a year and a half, Mrs. Judson's health began to break down under the effects of the climate. They had no physician to consult, and her symptoms proving dangerous, she was obliged to sail to Madras to secure both medical advice and the recuperation of a sea voyage. She set sail on January 25, 1815, and after an absence of nearly three months, returned with her health much improved.

This painful separation occasioned by Mrs. Judson's illness was closely followed by domestic bereavement. A little son, born September 11, 1815, and named Roger

Williams, died on the fourth of the following May, at the age of seven months and twenty-three days.

Following this, Mr. Judson himself was taken ill, after almost three years of the closest application to study. But even the hours of his illness he improved by formulating in a grammar the knowledge he had acquired of the language. Fearing that his own life might soon come to a close, he determined to *blaze* the trees through this hitherto untrodden wilderness of the Burmese language, by putting in permanent form the results of his own studies. On July 13, 1816, exactly three years to a day after his arrival, he completed a work with the modest title, "Grammatical Notices of the Burman Language," which proved of great value.

Partially recovering from his illness, Mr. Judson completed on July 30, 1816, his first tract, entitled, " A View of the Christian Religion, in three parts, Historic, Didactic, and Preceptive." The next step was to multiply this tract, and speed it on its way among the Burmans. A press and Burman types had already arrived—a valuable present from the English Baptist brethren of Serampore. A missionary printer, the Rev. Geo. H. Hough, and his wife, were already on their way from America. Mr. Rice was still arousing the Baptists in the United States to send on reinforcements of men and money.

The reinforcements at last arrived. On October 15, 1816, the Rev. Mr. Hough with his family landed at Rangoon, and upon his arrival he immediately put the printing press into operation. One thousand copies of the tract above mentioned, and three thousand copies of a catechism which had just been completed by Mrs. Judson, were struck off and put into circulation. This strange new religion could not fail of at least catching

the attention of the inquisitive Burmans. As the fisher-
men attach many hooks to a long line stretched across a
river, hoping that at least a few of the many fish swim-
ming past may be taken, so our missionaries with much
care and toil adjusted their trawl of tracts in the midst
of the dense Burmese population, and anxiously, prayer-
fully awaited the result.

On May 20, 1817, Mr. Judson completed the translation of the Gospel of Matthew. This marks the first
stage in the monumental task of translating the whole
Bible into Burmese. Two days later he began to com-
pile a Burman dictionary. But close application for
more than four years to the study of the Burman language, to the translation of tracts and Scriptures, and to
the compilation of a grammar and dictionary, was breaking down his health. A sea voyage was needed to restore
his vigor. But need of rest alone would not have caused
him to take even a few weeks' vacation from his toils
and cares. He was impatient to begin holding public
services in the Burman tongue. But although he understood the structure of the language, and could read,
write, and speak in Burman, yet for conducting public
worship he felt the need of a native Christian helper.

Burma is flanked on the western side by the mountains
of Arracan; between these and the bay of Bengal lies
the flat coast district of Chittagong. It had been ceded
to the English. The inhabitants of this district spoke
Burmese. A few years before, the English Baptists had
begun a mission in Chittagong. Several converts had
been baptized, when the mission was abandoned. Mr.
Judson conceived the plan of visiting Chittagong, in
order to gather together the scattered converts, instruct
them anew, and perhaps bring one or two of them to

help him in Rangoon. This would furnish him employment during the needed vacation. Besides, the rare
opportunity was afforded of going and returning in the
same ship, so that he would have to be absent for only
three months. This pet project of his was painfully frustrated, and the three months were stretched out into
almost two-thirds of a year. The voyage was attended
by peculiar horrors.

They had sailed for Chittagong, a passage which should
have been made in ten or twelve days at the longest. He
had, therefore, prepared himself for only a few weeks'
absence from home. When the vessel put in at Cheduba,
the nervous affection of his head and eyes, occasioned at
first by low diet, had so much increased by exhaustion
and lack of food that he was unable to go on shore.
When they approached the Coromandel coast, and again
encountered contrary winds, they were reduced to almost
the last extremity, and the constitution of Mr. Judson
sank under these accumulated hardships. The mouldy,
broken rice, which they picked up from native vessels,
and this in small quantities, with a limited supply of
water, was their sole sustenance for three or four weeks.
Here he was alone, in a state of passive, monotonous
suffering, with no one to share his privations, and nothing
to arouse his energies. His scanty wardrobe, prepared
for a trip of ten or twelve days, had been long since exhausted, and what with starvation, filth, pain, and dis-
couragement, he became unable to leave his berth. At
last he was attacked by a slow fever, and turning in dis-
gust from his little mess of dirty rice, he begged continually for water! water! water! without ever obtaining
enough to quench, even for a moment, his devouring
thirst. At length the little vessel came to anchor in the

mud of Masulipatam, some two or three miles from the low, uninviting beach, and the captain came to inquire if he would be taken on shore. The fact that they were near land seemed to him an incredible thing, a kind of dreamy illusion too fanciful to interest him. After some urging, however, he became sufficiently roused to pencil a note, which he addressed to "any English resident of Masulipatam," begging only for a place on shore to die. After a little while, one of the men came below to tell him that a boat was approaching from the shore. He now succeeded in crawling to the window of his cabin, from which he plainly distinguished in the rapidly moving boat, both the red coat of the military and the white jacket of the civilian. In the first thrill of joyful surprise, the sudden awakening of hope and pleasure, he threw himself on his knees and wept. Before his new friends were fairly on board, he had succeeded in gaining some little self-control. He used to say afterward, "The white face of an Englishman never looked to me so beautiful, so like my conception of what angel faces are, as when these strangers entered my cabin."

They were very much shocked at his visible wretchedness: he was haggard, unshaven, dirty, and so weak that he could with difficulty support his own weight. Their earnest cordiality was peculiarly grateful to him. One of the officers took him to his own house, supplied him from his own wardrobe, procured a nurse, whom, however, he had occasion to employ but a short time, and displayed throughout a generous hospitality which Dr. Judson never forgot.

But his anxieties and sufferings during this voyage were fully paralleled by those of the heroic woman whom he had left behind him at Rangoon. From

Christmas Day, 1817, until July 16, of the following
year, no word whatever came to Mrs. Judson from her
husband, from whom she had expected to be parted only
for a few weeks. She occupied part of her time teaching
about thirty Burman women whom she had gathered
together. A succession of disasters had swept over the
little mission. She alone faltered not. We catch a
gleam at Rangoon of that same fidelity and courage that
afterward burned so long and so steadily at Ava and
Oung-pen-la. The mission was harassed by government
persecution. It was rumored that the foreigners were to
be banished. The viceroy, who had been their steady
friend, was recalled to Ava, and the new viceroy was a
stranger to them. A menacing order summoned Mr.
Hough to the court house, with the message that " If he
did not tell all the truth relative to his situation in the
country, they would write with his heart's blood." Mrs.
Judson interceded in person, and by her own knowledge
of the language and her matchless womanly tact, con-
ciliated the viceroy. Asiatic cholera raged in Rangoon
and the death gong sounded all the day long. Rumors of
war between England and Burma filled the air. The
English ships one by one hastily weighed anchor and
slipped out of the harbor; only a single vessel remained
—the only way of escape. Her missionary associates,
the Houghs, determined to seize this last opportunity, and
fly from the country before it was too late. Against her
will they urged her on board; but her great nature rose
in its strength, and she insisted on going ashore. She tore
herself away and went back to the mission premises
alone. Her husband, if still alive, should not return and
find his mission station deserted, and himself in Burma
without a companion.

After this gloomy episode the prospects of the mission began to brighten. Mr. Hough, indeed, had gone to Calcutta, taking the printing press with him, so that for some time all the press-work of the mission had to be done there. But on September 19, 1818, Messrs. Colman and Wheelock, with their wives, arrived in Rangoon and joined the mission, to which meanwhile Mr. Judson had safely returned.

The time had now come when his long-cherished desire to hold public worship among the Burmans in their own tongue was to be gratified. The little chapel or *zayat* had been built. It was not simply a church, but a religious schoolhouse as well. It also afforded a convenient place of rendezvous where Mr. Judson could sit all the day long, attracting the attention of those who passed by, and often engaging them in religious conversation.

On April 4, 1819, even before the *zayat* was completed, the first public service was held. Mr. Judson was thirty-one years old, and had been in Rangoon nearly six years before he ventured to preach to a Burman audience in their own tongue. This marks an era in the history of the Burman mission; for it is a noteworthy fact that the institution of public worship was soon followed by the first of a series of conversions.

It was on June 27, 1819, about seven years and four months after Mr. Judson left America, and about six years after his arrival in Rangoon, that he was permitted to baptize the first Burman convert, Moung Nau. The secret of that sublime faith which enabled him to endure without a misgiving so many long weary years, sowing without the joy of seeing a single blade of grain, may be learned from the following lines, which he wrote in pencil on the inner cover of a book which he was using in the compilation of the Burman dictionary:

> In joy or sorrow, health or pain,
> Our course be onward still;
> We sow on Burma's barren plain,
> We reap on Zion's hill.

These words suggest the difficulties and sufferings that attended the commencement of public worship among the Burmans, and the progress of that religious movement which culminated in the beginning of Christianity in Burma—the baptism of the first three converts, Moung Nau, Moung Byaa, and Moung Thahlah; as well as the conversion of the humble fisherman, Moung Ing, and the learned philosopher, Moung Shwa-gnong. Just at this most interesting period, when three Burmans had been baptized and many others were inquiring into the new religion, a black cloud of persecution gathered over the heads of these young converts and their Christian teachers. The viceroy of Rangoon regarded with an unfavorable eye this attempt to introduce a new religion. When informed that a prominent Burman teacher was about to renounce the religion of the empire, he uttered the ominous sentence: "Inquire further." These words scattered the group of inquirers that had gathered about Mr. Judson as quickly as the lifted hand disperses a school of fish. The new converts, indeed, stood firm even under the peril of the confiscation of their goods, and the risk of torture and death; but the work came to a standstill. The inhabitants of Rangoon did not even dare to visit the foreign teacher. In these circumstances the boldest measure seemed to Mr. Judson the wisest. He determined to beard the lion in his lair. He resolved to go directly to Ava, the capital of Burma, and lay the whole matter at the feet of the emperor. If he could gain from the Burman monarch permission to propagate the Christian religion among his subjects, then he would be at once exempt from the annoyance and perscention inflicted by provincial underlings. If, on the other hand, he should fail, matters could not be made any worse, as news of this religious movement would soon get to the ears of the king.

Before Mr. Judson and Mr. Colman set out for Ava, the little group of missionaries was thinned by the departure of the Wheelocks. Only seven days after Mr. Wheelock arrived in Rangoon, while engaged in family worship, he had a hemorrhage, and on August 7, 1819, set sail for Bengal. After being thirteen days at sea, during a period of temporary delirium, he threw himself into the ocean. While Mrs. Wheelock was engaged in writing, and he apparently lying asleep, she heard the cabin door close. She looked around, saw that he was gone, sprang to the door, opened it, and discovered that he had vanished forever from her sight. The ship was sailing with such speed that no effort could be made to rescue him. The death of this young man was a great loss to the infant mission. His fervent piety, his sweet and uncomplaining spirit, and his devotion to the work of saving the heathen, had endeared him to his missionary associates. After mentioning in one of his letters that he and Mr. Colman had only one room each, he adds: "We prefer one room in Rangoon to six in Boston. We feel that we are *highly blessed.*"

CHAPTER VI

ON December 21, 1819, Mr. Judson and Mr. Colman, leaving their wives alone in Rangoon, began their journey up the Irawadi to Ava, the capital of the empire.

The journey was made by boat. The viceroy granted them a pass to go up to the Golden Feet, and to lift up their eyes to the Golden Face. After making arrangements for their wives' residence in town during their absence, they went on board their little craft, which was six feet wide in the middle and forty feet long. A temporary deck of bamboos was laid throughout, and on the hinder part of the boat the sides were raised with thin boards, and a covering of thatch and mats, so as to form two low rooms, in which they could sit and lie.

The company consisted of sixteen besides themselves: ten rowmen, a steersman, a head man—whose name was inserted in their passport, and who therefore derived a little authority from government—a steward or cook for the company—which place was filled by their trusty Moung Nau, their own cook—a Hindu washerman, and an Englishman, who having been unfortunate all his life, wished to try the service of his Burman majesty; and this last person might have been called the gunner, he having charge of several guns and blunderbusses, which were indispensable on account of the robbers that infested the river.

74

They had been much perplexed in fixing on a present for the emperor, without which no person unauthorized could appear in his presence. Their funds were evidently inadequate to the purchase of articles which would be valuable to him from a pecuniary point of view; when they considered also that there ought to be a congruity between the present and their character, they selected that book which they hoped to be allowed to translate under his patronage, the BIBLE, in six volumes, covered with gold leaf, in Burman style, and each volume enclosed in a rich wrapper. For presents to other members of government, they had taken cloth and other articles.

Thus manned and furnished they pushed off from the shores of Rangoon. At night they moored by the banks of Kyee-myen-daing. It was near this place that, a few days before one of the boats belonging to a late collector of Rangoon had been attacked by robbers, and the steersman and another man killed at a single shot. They felt unwilling to remain at this village, but found it necessary.

On the 30th, they reached Kah-noung, a considerable town, about ninety miles from Rangoon. Here they met a special officer from Bassein, with a detachment of men, sent in pursuit of a band of robbers who had lately made a daring attack on a large boat, wounded and beaten off the people, and taken plunder to the amount of fifteen hundred *ticals*. The commander offered them an escort for the journey of the day following, which lay through a dangerous tract of country; but they declined accepting, as they would have been obliged to give the people presents, without deriving any substantial assistance in the hour of danger. They however took all needful precautions and kept a strict watch at night.

On January the 25th, about a month after leaving Rangoon, they arrived at Ava, and saw in the distance the golden dome of the palace amid the glittering pagodas. They set out early on the following morning, called on Mr. G., late collector of Rangoon, and on Mr. R., who had formerly been collector, but was now out of favor.

Thence they entered the city, passed the palace, and repaired to the house of Mya-day-men, former viceroy of Rangoon, now one of the public ministers of State (*woongyee*). They gave him a valuable present, and another of less value to his wife, the lady who had formerly treated Mr. G. with so much politeness. They both received them very kindly, and appeared to interest themselves in their success. They however did not disclose their precise object, but only petitioned leave to behold the Golden Face. Upon this, his highness committed their business to Moung Yo, one of his favorite officers, and directed him to introduce them to Moung Zah, one of the private ministers of State (*a-twen-woon*), with the necessary orders. This particular favor of Mya-day-men prevented the necessity of their petitioning and feeing all the public ministers of State, and procuring formal permission from the high court of the empire.

In the evening, Moung Yo, who lived near their boat, called on them to say that he would conduct them on the morrow. They lay down in sleepless anxiety. To-morrow's dawn would usher in the most eventful day of their lives. To-morrow's eve would close on the bloom or the blight of their fondest hopes.

The next day they left the boat, and put themselves under the conduct of Moung Yo. He carried them first to Mya-day-men, as a matter of form; and there they learned that the emperor had been privately apprised of their arrival, and said, "Let them be introduced." They therefore proceeded to the palace.

At the outer gate they were detained a long time until the various officers were satisfied that they had a right to enter, after which they deposited a present for the private minister of State, Moung Zah, and were ushered into his apartments in the palace yard. He received them very pleasantly, and ordered them to sit before several governors and petty kings, who were waiting at his levee. They here, for the first time, disclosed their character and object—told him that they were missionaries, or "propagators of religion"; that they wished to appear before the emperor and present their sacred books, accompanied with a petition. He took the petition into his hand, looked over about half of it, and then familiarly asked some questions about their God and their religion, to which they replied. Just at this crisis, some one announced that the Golden Foot was about to advance; on which the minister hastily rose up and put on his robes of State, saying that he must seize the moment to present them to the emperor. They now found that they had unwittingly fallen on an unpropitious time, it being the day of the celebration of the late victory over the Kathays, and the very hour when his majesty was coming forth to witness the display made on the occasion. When the minister was dressed, he just said, "How can you propagate religion in this empire? But come along."

Their hearts sank at these inauspicious words. He conducted them through various splendor and parade until they ascended a flight of stairs, and entered a most magnificent hall. He directed them where to sit, and took his place on one side; the present was placed on the other; and Moung Yo and another officer of Mya-day-men sat a little behind. The scene to which they were now introduced really surpassed their expectation. The spacious extent of the hall, the number and magnitude of the pillars, the height of the dome, the whole completely covered with gold, presented a most grand and imposing spectacle. Very few were present, and those evidently great officers of State. Their situation prevented them from seeing the farther avenue of the hall; but the end where they sat opened to the parade which the emperor was about to inspect. They remained about five minutes, when every one put himself into the most respectful attitude, and Moung Yo whispered that his majesty had entered.

They looked through the hall as far as the pillars would allow, and presently caught sight of this modern Ahasuerus. He came forward unattended—in solitary grandeur—exhibiting the proud gait and majesty of an eastern monarch. His dress was rich, but not distinctive; and he carried in his hand the gold-sheathed sword, which seems to have taken the place of the sceptre of ancient times. But it was his high aspect and commanding eye that chiefly riveted their attention. He strided on. Every head excepting theirs was now in the dust. They remained kneeling, their hands folded, their eyes fixed on the monarch. When he drew near, they caught his attention. He stopped, partly turned toward them—
" Who are these ? "

" The teachers, great king," was the reply.

" What, you speak Burman—the priests that I heard of last night ? "   " When did you arrive ? "   " Are you teachers of religion ? "   " Are you like the Portuguese priest ? "   " Are you married ? "   " Why do you dress so ? "

These and some other similar questions they answered, when he appeared to be pleased with them, and sat down on an elevated seat, his hand resting on the hilt of his sword, and his eyes intently fixed on them. Moung Zah now began to read the petition; and it ran thus:

"The American teachers present themselves to receive the favor of the excellent king, the sovereign of land and sea. Hearing that, on account of the greatness of the royal power, the royal country was in a quiet and prosperous state, we arrived at the town of Rangoon, within the royal dominions, and having obtained leave of the governor of that town to come up and behold the Golden Face, we have ascended and reached the bottom of the Golden Feet. In the great country of America, we sustain the character of teachers and explainers of the contents of the sacred Scriptures of our religion. And since it is contained in those Scriptures that if we pass to other countries and preach and propagate religion great good will result, and both those who teach and those who receive the religion will be freed from future punishment and enjoy without decay or death the eternal felicity of heaven—that royal permission be given, that we, taking refuge in the royal power, may preach our religion in these dominions, and that those who are pleased with our preaching and wish to listen to and be guided by it, whether foreigners or Burmans, may be exempt from government molestation, they present themselves to receive the favor of the excellent king, the sovereign of land and sea."

The emperor heard this petition, and stretched out his hand. Moung Zah crawled forward and presented it. His majesty began at the top, and deliberately read it through. In the meantime, Mr. Judson gave Moung Zah an abridged copy of a tract which had given offense, in which every offensive sentence was corrected, and the whole put into the handsomest style and dress possible. After the emperor had perused the petition, he handed it back without saying a word, and took the tract. Their hearts now rose to God for a display of his grace. "O have mercy on Burma! Have mercy on her king."

But alas! the time was not yet come. He held the tract long enough to read the first two sentences, which asserted that there is one eternal God, who is independent of the incidents of mortality, and that beside him there is no God; and then with an air of indifference, perhaps disdain, he dashed it down to the ground. Moung Zah stooped forward, picked it up, and handed it to the missionaries. Moung Yo made a slight attempt to save them by unfolding one of the volumes which composed their present and displaying its beauty; but his majesty took no notice. Their fate was decided. After a few moments, Moung Zah interpreted his royal master's will in the following terms:

"Why do you ask for such permission? Have not the Portuguese, the English, the Mussulmans, and people of all other religions, full liberty to practise and worship according to their own customs? In regard to the objects of your petition, his majesty gives no order. In regard to your sacred books, his majesty has no use for them; take them away."

Something was now said about brother Colman's skill in medicine; upon which the emperor once more opened his mouth, and said, "Let them proceed to the residence of my physician, the Portuguese priest; let him examine whether they can be useful to me in that line, and report accordingly."

He then rose from his seat, strode on to the end of the hall, and there, after having dashed to the ground the first intelligence that he had ever received of the eternal God, his Maker, his Preserver, his Judge, he threw himself down on a cushion, and lay listening to the music, and gazing at the parade moving on before him.

As for the missionaries and their present, they were huddled up and hurried away without much ceremony. They passed out of the palace gates with much more facility than they had entered, and were conducted first to the house of Mya-day-men. There his officer reported their reception, but in as favorable terms as possible; and as his highness was not apprised of their precise object, their repulse appeared probably to him not so decisive as they knew it to be.

They were next conducted two miles through the heat of the sun and dust of the streets of Ava to the residence of the Portuguese priest. He very speedily ascertained that they were in possession of no wonderful secret which would secure the emperor from all disease and make him live forever; and they were accordingly allowed to take leave of the reverend inquisitor, and retreat to their boat.

At this stage of the business, notwithstanding the decided repulse they had received, they still cherished some hope of ultimately gaining their point. They regretted that a sudden interruption had prevented their explaining their objects to Moung Zah in that familiar and confidential manner which they had intended; and they determined therefore to make another attempt upon him in private.

The following day, early in the morning, they had the pleasure of seeing their friend Mr. G. coming to their

F

boat. It may not be amiss to mention that he was the collector who had been chiefly instrumental in relieving them from an exorbitant demand which, a few months before, had been made upon them in Rangoon. He now told them that he had heard of their repulse, but would not have them give up all hope; that he was particularly acquainted with Moung Zah, and would accompany them to his house a little before sunset, at an hour when he was accessible. This precisely accorded with their intentions.

In the afternoon, therefore, they called on Mr. G., and he went with them into the city. On the way they paid a visit to the wife of the then viceroy of Rangoon, whose eldest son had married the daughter of the emperor. They carried a present, and were of course kindly received.

Thence they went to the house of Moung Zah, some way beyond the palace. He received them with great coldness and reserve. The conversation, which they carried on chiefly through Mr. G., it is unnecessary to detail. Suffice it to say, that they ascertained beyond a doubt, that the policy of the Burman Government in regard to the toleration of any foreign religion, was precisely the same as that of the Chinese; that it was quite out of the question whether any of the subjects of the emperor who embraced a religion different from his own, would be exempt from punishment; and that Mr. Judson and his companion, in presenting a petition to that effect, had been guilty of a most egregious blunder, an unpardonable offense.

Mr. G. urged every argument they suggested, and some others. He finally stated that if they obtained the royal favor other foreigners would come and settle in the empire, and trade would be greatly benefited. This argument alone seemed to have any effect on the mind of the minister, and looking out from the cloud which covered his face he vouchsafed to say that if we would wait some time he would endeavor to speak to his majesty about them. From this remark it was impossible to derive any encouragement; and having nothing further to urge, they left Mr. G., and bowing down to the ground, took leave of this great minister of State who, under the emperor, guided the movements of the whole empire.

It was now evening. They had four miles to walk by moonlight. Arrived at the boat, they threw themselves down, completely exhausted in body and mind. For three days they had walked eight miles a day, the most of the way in the heat of the sun, which even at that season, in the interior of those countries, is exceedingly oppressive, and the result had been an apparent failure.

After making several more ineffectual attempts to reach the emperor, they began their return journey on February 6th, having spent two weeks in Ava without success. Sad at heart they descended the Irawadi, and after an uneventful journey of a fortnight, arrived in Rangoon, February 18th. They were utterly disheartened, for their journey had been a complete failure. The emperor had refused to give them permission to propagate the Christian religion among his subjects; and any Burman who should renounce Buddhism and become a Christian, would incur the displeasure of his sovereign.

Mr. Judson at once decided to remove the mission to Chittagong, where under the protection of the British flag he could preach Christ to a Burmese-speaking population. He gathered his converts and inquirers together, and made no concealment of the failure at Ava. He pictured the sufferings to which the Burman would be exposed who should espouse Christianity, while he declared his intention, reluctantly formed, of leaving the country. But to his great surprise his converts stood firm. They expressed their willingness to suffer persecution, and even death, rather than renounce Christ. They entreated him not to leave them. "Stay at least," they said, "until a little church of ten is collected, and a native teacher is set over it, and then, if you must go, we will not say nay. In that case we shall not be concerned. This religion will spread of itself. The emperor can not stop it." The heroism of the disciples prevailed to keep the teacher in Rangoon.

It was thought best, however, that Mr. Colman and his wife should go to Chittagong to gather together the few converts left there by the English Baptists, and to preach the gospel to the Arracanese. Thus Chittagong might prove an asylum for the Judsons and their Burman converts if they should be hunted out of Rangoon. On March 27, 1820, Mr. Colman embarked for Arracan, where after a short but heroic missionary career, he died at Cox's Bazaar, on the 4th of July, 1822.

Thus Mr. and Mrs. Judson again found themselves alone at Rangoon. The Houghs, the Wheelocks, the Colmans had gone. They were left with their group of three converts to continue the conflict with heathenism. But strange to say in this darkest hour of all the Spirit began to work mightily in the hearts of the Burmans. Within five months, in the very face of impending persecution, seven heathen, one after another, were converted and baptized, among them the learned, skeptical Moung Shwa-gnong, and the first woman, Mah-men-la. The church of three native converts rapidly grew into a church of ten. But at this point Mrs. Judson's health became so completely shattered that in order to save her life, Mr. Judson had to take her to Calcutta.

Mr. and Mrs. Judson embarked at Rangoon July 19, 1820, and arrived at Calcutta on the 18th of August. What a pang it must have cost them to leave their little mission just at this time when, after long years of waiting, they saw the Burmans eagerly and rapidly embracing the gospel!

The three months spent at Serampore, near Calcutta, caused a great improvement in Mrs. Judson's health. The two weary missionaries had sweet and restful intercourse with the English Baptists stationed there, and with "the affectionate family of Mr. Hough." Mr. Judson's enjoyment was only marred by his extreme anxiety about "those few sheep that I have left in the Burman wilderness." "Oh, may the great Shepherd," he prayed, "feed the little flock, and gather the lambs with his arm, and carry them in his bosom."

On November 23d, Mr. and Mrs. Judson embarked again for Rangoon, where they arrived January 5, 1821. Their voyage was tedious and distressing above any that they had ever taken. The brig was so small and so filled with native passengers that they were unable to obtain the least exercise by walking on deck, and it was so full of scorpions and centipedes that they never dared close their eyes to sleep without completely enfolding themselves with curtains. In addition to these inconveniences, they had a strong contrary wind, and frequently violent squalls, with the most terrific thunder and lightning they had ever witnessed. They were six weeks in making a passage which was generally made in ten or fifteen days. After their joyous arrival in Rangoon they plunged once more into their missionary work.

It now became Mr. Judson's painful duty to send his wife to America. This would occasion a separation of at least two years, but unless it was done the life so dear to him, and of such incalculable value to the Burman mission, would soon be brought to a close. In accord with this resolve, Mrs. Judson embarked for Calcutta, on her way to America, August 21, 1821. His letters written to his wife during her absence betray here and there a sinking of his buoyant spirits. Even while on her journey to her dear native land, Mrs. Judson cast " a longing, lingering look behind." It was hard to leave Rangoon, even to go to America.

She was heartily welcomed by the Christians of England, and was entertained at the house of Mr. Butterworth, a member of Parliament, who afterward referring to her in a public address said that her visit at his house reminded him of the words of Scripture : Be not forgetful to entertain strangers, for thereby some have entertained angels unawares. She arrived in America September 25, 1822, and remained until the 22d of June, 1823. Her visit in this country awakened great missionary enthusiasm, and on her return she was accompanied by two newly appointed missionaries, Mr. and Mrs. Wade. She reached Rangoon on the 5th of December, 1823, after an absence of about two years and three months, finding her husband having made appreciable advance in his work, and with still larger plans for the future.

After Mrs. Judson's departure, Mr. Judson had been left alone in Rangoon for nearly four months, and continued his labors in complete solitude. On December 31, 1821, the Rev. Jonathan Price, M. D., a medical missionary, arrived with his family and joined the mission. About a month later Mr. Hough and his family returned

from Calcutta. On the 2d of May, 1822, Mrs. Price
died, after having been in the country only five months,
and was buried by the side of Mr. Judson's little Roger.
Dr. Price's medical skill, especially shown in performing
operations for cataracts, attracted the attention of the
Burman emperor at Ava. He was summoned to appear
at the royal court, and Mr. Judson thought it best to
accompany him, hoping that now the king's favor might
be secured in behalf of the new religion, and that he
might even be permitted to plant a mission in the capital
city. So on August 28, 1822, Mr. Judson set out on his
second journey to Ava, this time in the company of Dr.
Price, and at the expense of the government. In the
meantime the number of the native church-membership
in Rangoon had grown from ten to eighteen.

Mr. Judson and Dr. Price spent five months in Ava,
returning to Rangoon in February, 1823. They were
kindly received by the emperor, who being impressed by
the medical knowledge of Dr. Price, invited them to
make their residence at the capital. The way now seemed
open to establish a mission in Ava. Mr. Judson always
longed to go into the "region beyond." The Houghs
and Wades could sufficiently care for the infant church
at Rangoon. Why not plant a church in the heart of the
empire, under the shelter of the throne?

But before going to Ava to execute his daring purpose
to plant a mission in the capital of Burma, he must
await Mrs. Judson's arrival. Ten months intervened
between his return from Ava and her arrival at Rangoon.
During this time he completed the translation of the
New Testament into Burmese, and prepared an epitome
of the Old Testament, which might serve as an introduc-
tion to the study of the New. On the 13th of December,

1823, eight days after Mrs. Judson's arrival, he set out in company with her for Ava, where they arrived on January 23, 1824. This marked an epoch in Mr. Judson's life. His ardent, active temperament was to be subjected to the crucible of passive endurance; and we now pass from the record of his activities to the story of his sufferings.

CHAPTER VII

LIFE IN AVA AND OUNG—PEN—LA. 1823-1826

WHEN Mr. and Mrs. Judson left Rangoon to establish their home in Ava, the outlook was encouraging. They had left behind them a small but vigorous church of eighteen converted Burmans, under the care of Mr. and Mrs. Hough and Mr. and Mrs. Wade. They had been invited by the king to live in the capital city, and had received from him a plot of ground on which to build a mission house. They felt sure of royal protection and favor. Many persons of high rank seemed kindly disposed to the new religion; while Dr. Price had won golden opinions by his medical skill. They immediately commenced the building of a little dwelling-house, and Mrs. Judson soon had a school of three native girls. Mr. Judson preached in Burmese every Sunday at Dr. Price's house, and held worship every evening.

A dark cloud, however, was gathering on the horizon. War was impending between Burma and the English government in India. For two years the Christians of America were kept in a state of terrible suspense, unbroken by any tidings from their missionaries in Ava, which was only assuaged by fervent and universal prayer on their behalf.

The occasion of the war was Chittagong, that particular strip of low land lying along the sea and flanking Burma on the west, to which Mr. Colman had gone to

prepare an asylum for the Judsons, in case they should
be driven out of Rangoon. This district was under
British rule, and refugees from the cruel despotism of
Burma had taken shelter there. The Burman monarch
insisted that his victims should be arrested by the
English authorities and handed over to him. Besides,
he felt that Chittagong belonged naturally to Burma.
And such was his pride and his contempt for British
prowess, that he deemed it quite possible for him not
only to recover this territory, but even to conquer the
whole of Bengal.

When war actually broke out, suspicion fell at once
on all the white foreigners residing in Ava. They were
thought to be spies secretly acting in collusion with the
English government. They were immediately arrested,
fettered, and thrown into the death prison.

"I was seized," Dr. Judson writes, "on the 8th of
June, 1824, in consequence of the war with Bengal, and
in company with Dr. Price, three Englishmen, one
American, and one Greek, was thrown into the death
prison at Ava, where we lay eleven months—nine months
in three pairs, and two months in five pairs of fetters.
The scenes we witnessed and the sufferings we underwent
during that period I would fain consign to oblivion.
From the death prison at Ava we were removed to a
country prison at Oung-pen-la, ten miles distant, under
circumstances of such severe treatment, that one of our
number, the Greek, expired on the road; and some of
the rest, among whom was myself, were scarcely able
to move for several days. It was the intention of the
government in removing us from Ava, to have us sacri-
ficed in order to insure victory over the foreigners; but
the sudden disgrace and death of the adviser of that

measure prevented its execution. I remained in the
Oung-pen-la prison six months in one pair of fetters;
at the expiration of which period I was taken out of
irons, and sent under a strict guard to the Burmese headquarters at Mah-looan, to act as interpreter and translator.
Two months more elapsed, when on my return to Ava, I
was released at the instance of Moung Shwa-loo, the
north governor of the palace, and put under his charge.
During the six weeks that I resided with him the affairs
of the government became desperate, the British troops
making steady advances on the capital; and after Dr.
Price had been twice dispatched to negotiate for peace (a
business which I declined as long as possible), I was
taken by force and associated with him. We found the
British above Pah-gan; and on returning to Ava with
their final terms, I had the happiness of procuring the
release of the very last of my fellow-prisoners; and on
the 21st instant, obtained the reluctant consent of the
government to my final departure from Ava with Mrs.
Judson."

In these few modest words Mr. Judson passes over all the
prolonged horrors which he endured in the confinement
of an Oriental jail. Let us glance at his experience more
in detail. His imprisonment was remarkable for its
duration. For nine months he was confined in three
pairs of fetters, two months in five, six months in one;
for two months he was a prisoner at large; and for
nearly two months, although released from prison, he was
yet restrained in Ava under the charge of the north
governor of the palace, so that his confinement reached
nearly to the end of twenty-one long months.

Again, for most of the time of his confinement he was
shut up in a loathsome, wretched place. It derived its

remarkable, well-selected name, *Let-ma-yoon*—literally interpreted, *Hand, shrink not*—from the revolting scenes of cruelty practised within its walls. To those acquainted with the Burmese language the name conveys a peculiar impression of terror. It contemplates the extreme of human suffering, and when this has reached a point at which our nature recoils—when it is supposed that any one bearing the human form might well refuse to be the instrument to add to it, the hand of the executioner is apostrophized and encouraged not to follow the dictates of the heart: "Thine eye shall not pity and thine hand not spare." [1]

The Let-ma-yoon was a building about forty feet long and thirty feet wide. It was five or six feet high along the sides, but as the roof sloped, the center of it was perhaps double that height. There was no ventilation except through the chinks between the boards and through the door, which was generally closed. On the thin roof poured the burning rays of a tropical sun. In this room were confined nearly one hundred prisoners of both sexes and all nationalities. Dr. Price thus describes the impressions he received on entering the prison:

"A little bamboo door opened, and I rose to go toward it. But oh! who can describe my sensations? shackled like a common felon in the care of hangmen the offscouring of the country, turned like a dog into his kennel, my wife, my dear family, left to suffer alone all the rudeness such wretches are capable of. The worst, however, was yet to come; for making the best of my way up the high steps, I was ushered into the grand apartment. Horror of horrors, what a sight! never to my dying day shall I forget the scene: a dim lamp in the midst, just making

---

[1] See Gouger's "Narrative of Imprisonment in Burma."

darkness visible, and discovering to my horrified gaze
sixty or seventy wretched objects, some in long rows
made fast in the stocks, some strung on long poles, some
simply fettered; but all sensible of a new acquisition of
misery in the approach of a new prisoner. Stupefied, I
stopped to gaze, till goaded on, I proceeded toward the
farther end, when I again halted. A new and unexpected
sight met my eyes. Till now I had been kept in ignorance of the fate of my companions. A long row of
white objects, stretched on the floor in a most crowded
situation, revealed to me however but too well their sad
state, and I was again urged forward. Poor old Rodgers,
wishing to retain the end of the bamboo, made way for
me to be placed alongside of Mr. Judson.

"'We all hoped you would have escaped, you were so
long coming,' was the first friendly salutation I had yet
received; but alas, it was made by friends whose sympathy was now unavailing."

The following description of the interior of this jail is
given by an English fellow-prisoner of Mr. Judson:

"The only articles of furniture the place contained
were these: First, and most prominent, was a gigantic
row of stocks, similar in its construction to that formerly
used in England, but now nearly extinct, though dilapi-
dated specimens may still be seen in some of the market-
places of our own country towns. It was capable of
accommodating more than a dozen occupants, and like
a huge alligator opened and shut its jaws with a loud
snap upon its prey. Several smaller reptiles, interesting
varieties of the same species, lay basking around this
monster, each holding by the leg a pair of hapless victims consigned to its custody. There were heavy logs of
timber, bored with holes to admit the feet, and fitted with

wooden pins to hold them fast. In the center of the apartment was placed a tripod, holding a large earthen cup filled with earth-oil, to be used as a lamp during the night-watches; and lastly, a simple but suspicious looking piece of machinery whose painful uses it was my fate to test before many hours had elapsed. It was merely a long bamboo suspended from the roof by a rope at each end, and worked by blocks or pulleys, to raise or depress it at pleasure.

"Before me, stretched on the floor, lay forty or fifty hapless wretches, whose crimes or misfortunes had brought them into this place of torment. They were all nearly naked, and the half-famished features and skeleton frames of many of them too plainly told the story of their protracted sufferings. Very few were without chains, and some had one or both feet in the stocks besides. A sight of such squalid wretchedness can hardly be imagined. Silence seemed to be the order of the day; perhaps the poor creatures were so engrossed with their own misery that they hardly cared to make any remarks on the intrusion of so unusual an inmate as myself.

"The prison had never been washed, nor even swept, since it was built. So I was told, and have no doubt it was true, for, besides the ocular proof from its present condition, it is certain no attempt was made to cleanse it during my subsequent tenancy of eleven months. This gave a kind of fixedness or permanency to the fetid odors, until the very floors and walls were saturated with them, and joined in emitting the pest. As might have been expected from such a state of things, the place was teeming with creeping vermin to such an extent that very soon reconciled me to the plunder of the greater portion of my dress."

Surely it was enough for Mr. Judson to be shut up in the hot, stifling stench of a place like this without having his ankles and legs weighted with five pairs of irons, the scars from which he wore to his dying day. He could say with the Apostle Paul, " I bear in my body the marks of the Lord Jesus." In each pair of fetters the two iron rings were connected by a chain so short that the heel of one foot could hardly be advanced to the toe of the other ; and this task could be accomplished only by "shuffling a few inches at a time." The five pairs of irons weighed about fourteen pounds, and when they were removed after being long worn, there was a strained sensation, the equilibrium of the body seemingly being destroyed, so that the head was too heavy for the feet. Then at nightfall, lest the prisoners should escape, they were "*strung*" on a bamboo pole.

"When night came on," writes one of Mr. Judson's fellow-prisoners, "the 'Father' of the establishment, entering, stalked toward our corner. The meaning of the bamboo now became apparent. It was passed between the legs of each individual, and when it had threaded our number, seven in all, a man at each end hoisted it up by the blocks to a height which allowed our shoulders to rest on the ground, while our feet depended from the iron rings of the fetters. The adjustment of the height was left to the judgment of our kind-hearted parent, who stood by to see that it was not high enough to endanger life, nor low enough to exempt from pain. . . . In the morning, our considerate parent made his appearance, and with his customary grin, lowered the bamboo to within a foot of the floor, to the great relief of our benumbed limbs, in which the blood slowly began again to circulate."

When Mr. Judson was subjected to these indignities and tortures, he was in the very prime of life—thirty-six years old. He had come to that age when a good physical constitution is thoroughly seasoned and well qualified to endure hardship. He had always taken the best care of his health. Even before leaving America, he had adopted the following rules: First, frequently to inhale large quantities of air, so as to expand the lungs to the uttermost; secondly, daily to sponge the whole body in cold water; and thirdly, and above all, to take systematic exercise in walking.

Again, he had that tough, wiry physique which endures unexpectedly even during prolonged crises. All this was in his favor. But, on the other hand, he was a student, unused to suffering hardship. His naturally vigorous constitution had been somewhat enfeebled by ten years of close application to study in a tropical climate, and of late years it had been completely shattered by repeated attacks of fever and ague. He was reared in the cold, bracing air of New England, and during the tedious hours of imprisonment, how often must his memory have projected the sufferings of the Oriental jail against the background of the cool, green hillsides of his childhood!

He was possessed moreover of an active, methodical nature, to which the enforced idleness of twenty-one months must have brought the keenest torture. There was his Burman Bible unfinished, and ten years of work in Rangoon going to pieces in his absence. He longed to be preaching the gospel. Now that he had at last completely mastered the native tongue, he was filled with Jeremiah's consuming zeal: "His word was in mine heart, and a burning fire shut up in my bones."

Endowed with a nervous temperament, his nature was exceedingly sensitive to discomfort. One of his fellow-prisoners says: "His painful sensitiveness to anything gross or uncleanly, amounting almost to folly, was an unfortunate virtue to possess, and made him live a life of constant martyrdom."

A nature amply endowed with these fine sensibilities must have instinctively shrunk from the filth of the dungeon and the squalor of the prisoners; while the constrained and crowded position, night and day, and the galling fetters were almost unendurable.

There was also much to shock his moral nature. He found himself thrown into close association with the basest criminals of the Burman capital. His pure look rested upon their repulsive features, his reluctant ears were filled with their vulgar and blasphemous jests. Besides this, again and again he saw the wretched prisoner tortured with the cord and mallet, and was forced to hear the writhing victim's shriek of anguish.

He was likewise a man of the strongest and tenderest affections. What keen mental anguish must he have experienced at the thought of his beloved wife threading alone the hot, crowded streets, hourly exposed to the insults of rude Burman officials; day by day bringing or sending food to the jail; assuaging the wretchedness of the prisoners by bribing their keepers; pleading for the release of her husband with one Burman officer after another, and with such pathetic eloquence that on one occasion she melted to tears even the old governor of the prison; carrying her little Maria all the way in her arms to that place never to be forgotten, Oung-pen-la, her only conveyance a rough cart, the violent motion of which, together with the dreadful heat and dust, made

her almost distracted; nursing her infant and the little
native girls under her care through a course of small-pox;
and at last, breaking down herself and brought to death's
door by the same loathsome disease, succeeded by the
dread spotted fever!

Add to these horrors of Mr. Judson's imprisonment
the daily and even hourly anticipation of torture and
death, and it will be difficult to conceive of a denser
cloud of miseries than that which settled down on his
devoted head. The prisoners knew that they were arrested as spies. The Burman king and his generals were
exasperated by the rapid and unexpected successes of the
English army, and Mr. Judson and his fellow-prisoners
had every reason to suppose that this pent-up fury would
be poured upon their heads. It was customary to *question*
the prisoner with instruments of torture—the cord and
the iron mallet. Rumors of a frightful doom were con-
stantly sounding in their ears. Now they heard their
keepers during the night sharpening the knives to de-
capitate the prisoners the next morning; now the roar
of their mysterious fellow-prisoner, a huge, starving lion-
ess, convinced them that they were to be executed by
being thrown into her cage; now it was reported that
they were to be burned up together with their prison as
a sacrifice; now that they were to be buried alive at the
head of the Burman army in order to insure its victory
over the English. The following description by Mr.
Gouger of the solemn hour of three, shows the exquisite
mental torture to which the prisoners were subjected:

"Within the walls nothing worthy of notice occurred
until the hour of three in the afternoon. As this hour
approached, we noticed that the talking and jesting of the
community gradually died away; all seemed to be under

the influence of some powerful restraint, until that fatal hour was announced by the deep tones of a powerful gong suspended in the palace-yard, and a death-like silence prevailed. If a word was spoken it was in a whisper. It seemed as though even breathing was suspended under the control of a panic terror, too deep for expression, which pervaded every bosom. We did not long remain in ignorance of the cause. If any of the prisoners were to suffer death that day, the hour of three was that at which they were taken out for execution. The very manner of it was the acme of cold-blooded cruelty. The hour was scarcely tolled by the gong when the wicket opened, and the hideous figure of a spotted man appeared, who without uttering a word walked straight to his victim, now for the first time probably made acquainted with his doom. As many of these unfortunate people knew no more than ourselves the fate that awaited them, this mystery was terrible and agonizing; each one fearing, up to the last moment, that the stride of the spotted terror might be directed his way. When the culprit disappeared with his conductor, and the prison door closed behind them, those who remained began again to breathe more freely; for another day, at least, their lives were safe.

"I have described this process just as I saw it practised. On this first day, two men were thus led away in total silence; not a useless question was asked by the one party, nor explanation given by the other; all was too well understood. After this inhuman custom was made known to us, we could not but participate with the rest in their diurnal misgivings, and shudder at the sound of the gong and the apparition of the *pahquet*. It was a solemn daily lesson of an impressive character, 'Be ye also ready.'"

It is no wonder that Mr. Judson, in the midst of these horrors, took refuge in the quietism of Madame Guyon, and used often to murmur her beautiful lines:

> No place I seek, but to fulfill
> In life and death thy lovely will;
> No succor in my woes I want,
> Except what thou art pleased to grant.
> Our days are numbered—let us spare
> Our anxious hearts a needless care;
> ' Tis thine to number out our days,
> And ours to give them to thy praise.

CHAPTER VIII

LIFE IN AMHERST. 1826–1827

THE treaty of peace was signed by the British and Burmese Commissioners on the 24th of February, 1826. On the sixth of the following month, Mr. and Mrs. Judson, with the infant Maria, left the English army encamped at Yan-ta-bo. They sailed down the Irawadi in a British gunboat, and arrived at Rangoon March 21, 1826. Having at last emerged from the long nightmare of Oriental imprisonment, Mr. Judson turned to his life-work with undiminished ardor. The English desired to retain his valuable services as interpreter, and offered him a salary equivalent to three thousand dollars. But the offer was declined. Like the late Professor Agassiz, he had "no time to make money."

Mr. Judson had rapidly recovered from his imprisonment, and was now in perfect health.

"Even little Maria," he writes, "who came into the world a few months after my imprisonment to aggravate her parents' woes, and who has been, from very instinct it would seem, a poor, sad, crying thing, begins to brighten up her little face, and be somewhat sensible of our happy deliverance."

Missionary reinforcements had already come from America. Mr. Wade, while waiting in Calcutta for the war to close, was joined by George Dana Boardman, whose brief and saintly career was destined to make his name peculiarly fragrant to American Christians. He

seemed an ideal missionary, so completely was he fitted
for his work by his scholarly tastes, affectionate disposition, and fervent piety. He had taken up a newspaper a
little while before, and had seen a notice of Colman's un-
timely death in Arracan. In the twinkling of an eye
there flashed through his mind the question and answer:
" Who will go to fill his place ? " "*I* will go."

He had married Sarah Hall, a native of Salem, Massachusetts. Those who knew her speak of " faultless
features, molded on the Grecian model, beautiful transparent skin, warm, meek blue eyes, and soft hair, brown
in the shadow and gold in the sun." She was pronounced
by her English friends in Calcutta to be "the most
finished and faultless specimen of an American woman
that they had ever known." From her earliest years she
had possessed an enthusiasm for missions. When ten
years old, she wrote a poem upon the death at Rangoon
of Mrs. Judson's infant, Roger. Little did the child
dream that many years after she was to take the place of
the ideal heroine of her childhood, who, worn out with
the prolonged horrors of Ava and Oung-pen-la, lay
down to rest beneath the hopia-tree at Amherst.

Mr. Wade and Mr. Boardman waited anxiously in
Calcutta for news from the Judsons. They did not, however, wait in idleness. They were learning the Burman
language as best they could, and preaching in English in
the Circular Road Baptist Chapel, where they were permitted to see, as a result of their labors, many persons
converted and baptized. When news came at last from
Mr. Judson, they were ready to join him and labor wherever he should think it best.

But to return to Mr. Judson in Rangoon. Not only
did he find that the white teachers and their wives had

been driven away by the war, but the native church-membership was much reduced. He had left a church of eighteen disciples. He found on his return only four. With the exception of two, none however had disgraced their holy profession. The learned teacher, Moung Shwa-gnong, had gone into the interior of the country, and soon afterward died of the cholera. The only four whom Mr. Judson could muster after the war had swept over Rangoon, were Moung Shwa-ba, who had remained at the mission house, Moung Ing, who with such fidelity served Mrs. Judson through all her long, bittter experiences at Ava, and two faithful women, Mah-men-la and Mah-doke, who had been living in boats at Prome, the half-way place between Rangoon and Ava, and who instantly resolved to accompany the Judsons to Rangoon. These four faithful disciples were ready to follow their white teacher wherever he should think it best to establish a mission.

It was out of the question to think of remaining at Rangoon. The English were only holding the place temporarily, until the Burmans should pay their war debt. Indeed, at the close of the year, the English army did vacate Rangoon, and the Burmans resumed possession of their chief seaport. Should the missionaries therefore remain in Rangoon, they would still be under the cruel sway of Burman despotism. In addition, the monarch at Ava was peculiarly exasperated with his subjects in the southern part of the empire, because they had put themselves under the benignant protection of the English; many of the peaceful inhabitants were no doubt to be massacred by the royal troops. A state of anarchy followed the war. A famine succeeded, in which beasts of prey became proportionally bold. Tigers began to infest the suburbs of Rangoon, and carry off cattle and human beings. A tiger was killed even in the streets of the city. All these circumstances impelled the missionaries to leave Rangoon.

It was now no longer necessary for them to remain there in order to reach the native Burmans. One of the results of the war was that the British had wrested from the Burmans a large part of their seacoast, the Tenasserim provinces having been ceded to them. These embraced a strip of country along the sea, five hundred miles long, and from forty to eighty miles wide. This country was peopled with Burmans, and the cruelty of the despot at Ava was sure to cause a large overflow of the population of Burma proper into it. Here the Judsons might teach the new religion unmolested, under the protection of the British flag.

But where upon this long strip of ceded territory should the mission be established? Just at this time Mr. Judson was invited by Mr. Crawford, the British civil commissioner of the new province, to accompany him on an exploring expedition. The purpose of the expedition was to ascertain the best location for a town, which was to be the capital of the new territory—the seat of government and the headquarters of the army. Mr. Judson's acquaintance with the language of the Burmans made him an invaluable assistant in such an enterprise; and finally Mr. Judson and Mr. Crawford selected as the site for the new city the promontory where the waters of the Salwen empty themselves into the sea. "The climate was salubrious, the land high and bold to the seaward, and the view of the distant hills of Ballou Island very captivating." The town, in honor of the Governor-General of India, was named Amherst.

On July 2, 1826, Mr. and Mrs. Judson began their missionary life in Amherst. They had the four faithful Rangoon converts as the nucleus of a native church, and expected soon to be joined by Mr. and Mrs. Wade and Mr. and Mrs. Boardman. They were among the first settlers, and made their home right in the very jungle. There was a prospect that the new town would have a very rapid growth. Three hundred Burmans had just arrived, and reported that three thousand more were on their way in boats. It would not seem strange if in two or three years a city of twenty or thirty thousand inhabitants should spring up on this salubrious, wooded promontory.

But before missionary operations were fairly begun, Mr. Judson was compelled reluctantly to visit Ava, the scene of his imprisonment. The English Government desired to negotiate a commercial treaty with the Burman king, and Mr. Crawford, the civil commissioner of the newly ceded provinces, was appointed envoy. He invited Mr. Judson to accompany him as a member of the embassy. The missionary's profound knowledge of the Burman language and character well qualified him for the delicate and difficult task of treating with the court at Ava. At first he firmly declined. He had no relish for diplomatic occupation, and he longed to plunge again into his own work. But when he was assured that if he would go as an English ambassador every effort would be made to secure the insertion of a clause in the treaty granting religious liberty to the Burmans, so that the whole country would be thrown open to the gospel, he reluctantly consented. The stubborn intolerance of the native government had hitherto been the chief obstacle in his missionary work, and religious freedom for the Burmese was a

blessing for which he had long prayed and striven in
vain.

This step, which proved to be a most unfortunate one,
was, however, the result of the most mature deliberation.
Mr. Judson, with the English embassy, arrived at Ava
September 30, 1826, and remained there about two months
and a half. This period embraces one of the saddest
periods of his life. He was forced to witness the scene
of his prolonged sufferings in prison, and yet was separated from the wife and babe who had shared with him
those horrible experiences. He was engaged in the
tedious and uncongenial task of wrestling as a diplomat
with the stupidity and intolerance of the Burmese court.
He soon learned that the king would on no terms agree
to a clause in the treaty granting his subjects freedom of
worship. And to crown his sorrows, on the 4th of November there was placed in his hands a sealed letter, containing the intelligence that Mrs. Judson was no more.

After the departure of her husband for Amherst she
had begun her work with good heart. She built a little
bamboo dwelling-house and two schoolhouses. In one
of these she gathered ten Burman children, who were
placed under the instruction of faithful Moung Ing,
while she herself assembled the few native converts for
public worship every Sunday.

But in the midst of these sacred toils she was smitten
with fever. Her constitution, undermined by the hardships and sufferings which she had endured, could not
sustain the shock, and on October 24th, 1826, in the
thirty-seventh year of her age, she breathed her last.
The hands so full of holy endeavors were destined to be
suddenly folded for rest. She died apart from him to
whom she had given her heart in her girlhood, whose

footsteps she had faithfully followed for fourteen years, over land and sea, through trackless jungles and strange crowded cities, sharing his studies and his privations, illumining his hours of gloom with her beaming presence, and with a heroism and fidelity unparallelled in the annals of missions, soothing the sufferings of his imprisonment. He whom she had thus loved, and who, from his experience of Indian fever, might have been able to avert the fatal stroke, was far away in Ava. No missionary was with her when she died to speak words of Christian consolation. The Burman converts like children gathered helplessly and broken-hearted about their *white mamma.* The hands of strangers smoothed her dying pillow, and their ears received her last faint wandering utterances. Under such auspices as these her white-winged spirit took its flight to the brighter scenes of the New Jerusalem.

Mr. Judson returned to Amherst, January 24, 1827. The native Christians greeted him with the voice of lamentation, for his presence reminded them of the great loss they had sustained in the death of Mrs. Judson. His heart was desolate. His motherless babe had been tenderly cared for by Mrs. Wade. Mr and Mrs. Wade had arrived from Calcutta about two months before, and with them Mr. Judson made his temporary home. Two months later Mr. and Mrs. Boardman arrived, so that the missionary force was increased to five. The little native church of four members was however reduced by the departure of Moung Ing. This poor fisherman, who had been Mrs. Judson's faithful companion at Ava, had of his own accord conceived the purpose of undertaking a missionary excursion to his late fishing-grounds, Tavoy and Mergui, towns south of Amherst, situated on the Tenasserim coast. He was henceforth to be a fisher of men.

Mr. Boardman, in speaking of his first meeting with Mr. Judson, said: "He looks as if worn out with sufferings and sorrows." He did not, however, neglect his missionary work. He met the Burmans for public worship on Sunday, and each day at family worship new inquirers stole in and were taught the religion of Christ. He was also busily employed in revising the New Testament in several points which were not satisfactorily settled when the translation was made; for his besetting sin was, as he himself describes it, "a lust for finishing." He completed two catechisms for the use of Burman schools, the one astronomical, the other geographical, while his sorrowful heart sought comfort in commencing a translation of the book of Psalms.

Little Maria was the solace of his studies. But she too was taken from him. "On April 24, 1827," he writes, "my little daughter Maria breathed her last, aged two years and three months, and her emancipated spirit fled, I trust, to the arms of her fond mother."

Mr. Boardman, who had only just arrived from Calcutta, constructed a coffin, and made all the preparations for the funeral. At nine o'clock the next day little Maria was placed by her mother's side beneath the hopia-tree. "After leaving the grave," Mr. Boardman writes, "we had a delightful conversation on the kindness and tender mercies of our Heavenly Father. Brother Judson seemed carried above his grief."

And so at the age of thirty-nine he found himself alone in the world, bereft of his wife and two children.

The time had now come when the little mission established at Amherst, with such doleful omens, was to be broken up. Amherst was being rapidly eclipsed by the town of Moulmein, situated on the coast about twenty-five miles farther north, at the very mouth of the Salwen. Moulmein was also a new town, the settlers building their houses right in a thick jungle. But within a year of the first settlement, while the number of houses in Amherst amounted to two hundred and thirty and the population to twelve hundred, the population of Moulmein had rapidly swelled to twenty thousand. The reason for this growth was an unfortunate misunderstanding between the civil commissioner, Mr. Crawford, and the commander-in-chief, Sir Archibald Campbell.

The latter made Moulmein instead of Amherst the headquarters of his army. He regarded Moulmein as a more strategical position. The harbor too, of Amherst, though spacious and capable of accommodating ships of large burden, was difficult of access, and being farther out from the mouth of the Salwen than Moulmein, was dangerous during the southwest monsoon. The presence of the commander-in-chief and of his army at Moulmein, naturally attracted emigration thither, and it soon became apparent that this town instead of Amherst was to be the metropolis of the ceded provinces of Tennasserim. Accordingly it seemed best to transfer the mission to Moulmein. On May 28, 1827, Mr. and Mrs. Boardman removed thither from Amherst, and took possession of a frail bamboo mission house situated about a mile south of the cantonments of the English army. The site for the mission had been presented by Sir Archibald Campbell. "It was a lonely spot, and the thick jungle close at hand was the haunt of wild beasts whose howls sounded dismally on their ears in the night time."

On the 10th of August Mr. Judson left Amherst, and

the little enclosure, the hopia-tree, and the graves which contained the mouldering remains of those who were dearest to him on earth. He joined the Boardmans at Moulmein, and on the 14th of November was followed by Mr. and Mrs. Wade, and the native Christians, together with thirteen native school children. Mah-men-la, however, the first female convert among the Burmans, had already been laid to rest by the side of her *white mamma.* Sorrows do not come as single spies, but by battalions. Six months intervened between · the deaths of Mrs. Judson and little Maria, and within three months of the burial of the latter, even before leaving Amherst, Mr. Judson heard of the death of his venerable father, who departed this life at Scituate, Massachusetts, November 26, 1826, in the seventy-fifth year of his age

CHAPTER IX

MR. JUDSON was now forty years old. He had come to middle life, when one is no longer young, nor yet old—a time when one naturally looks both before and after. At nineteen years of age he was graduated from college; at twenty he was converted; at twenty-two he resolved to become a missionary to the heathen; at twenty-four he was married to Ann Hasseltine and embarked for India; at twenty-five he arrived in Rangoon; at thirty-one he baptized the first Burman convert; at thirty-five he completed the translation of the New Testament into Burmese; at thirty-six he was fettered and imprisoned at Ava; at thirty-eight he heard the news of Mrs. Judson's death at Amherst; and at thirty-nine buried his little Maria by the side of her mother under the hopia-tree. He found himself alone, and might naturally have asked himself the question, "What have I to show for what I have done and suffered?" Many of his fondest hopes had been shattered. His family was gone. His little church at Rangoon was all but extinct. Very few Burmans had learned to believe in the living God. The deep shadow of loneliness pervades all of his letters written during this period.

His sadness was intensified by the slowness of American Christians in sending on reinforcements. He often felt that he had been left out on the skirmish line almost alone. A letter written after his death, by his surviving

widow, shows how intense was his longing for the sympathy
and co-operation of his brethren at home. " I cannot
regret that Dr. Judson has gone. I believe it would have
broken his heart to see Burma open and such a lack of
missionary spirit. God spared him the trial, and though
it has left me so very desolate, I feel a sort of gladness
too, when I think of it. I suppose he sees it there, but
he can understand it better."

The transition period from Amherst to Moulmein must
have been a time of crisis. He was no longer stirred by
the enthusiasm of youth His constitution too had been
impaired by the prolonged tortures of Ava and Oung-
pen-la. He was alone. But his hardy nature did not
dissolve in the alembic of despair. While at times he
seemed to draw perilously near the verge of ascetic piet-
ism, his healthy spirit soon recovered its equilibrium. He
found his solace in new activities, and in a more intense
self-denial. His piety was not professional or obtrusive.
Mrs. E. C. Judson writes:

"I was first attracted by the freshness, the *originality*,
if I may so call it, of his goodness. . . His religion
mingled in his letters generally, and in his conversation—
a little silver thread that it is impossible to disentangle."

He was a man of prayer. His habit was to walk while
engaged in private prayer. One who knew him most intimately says that "His best and freest time for meditation and prayer was while walking rapidly in the open
air. He, however, attended to the duty in his room, and
so well was this peculiarity understood that when the
children heard a somewhat heavy, quick, but well-
measured tread, up and down the room, they would say,
'Papa is praying.'"

During this period of sickness, sorrow, and solitude, his

religion carried him to great extremes of self-denial. He was allowed by the governor-general of India five thousand two hundred rupees,[1] in consideration of his services at the treaty of Yandaboo and as a member of the embassy to Ava. Besides this, the presents he received while at Ava amounted to two thousand rupees.[2] All this money he paid into the treasury of the mission. Nor did he regard this as a donation. His view was that whatever a missionary might earn by such necessary and incidental outside work belonged, in the nature of the case, to the Board by which he was employed. Yet not only did he cheerfully give up these perquisites, but at a single stroke transferred to the mission all of his private property, the slow accumulation of many years of thrift.

But love of money was not the only worldly appetite which he nailed to the cross. He cut to the quick that passion for fame which was an inborn trait, and which had been inordinately stimulated by his parents during his earliest childhood. His overweening ambition received its first mortal wound, as he often remarked, when he became a Baptist. He declined the honorary degree of Doctor of Divinity conferred upon him by the corporation of Brown University in 1823.

The difficulty of writing his biography is enhanced by the fact that he destroyed, as far as possible, all his correspondence, including a letter of thanks for his services from the governor-general of India, and other papers of a similar kind. He seemed determined that his friends should have no material with which to construct eulogiums. He wanted to do his work and then forget all about it, and have every one else also forget it.

Again, Mr. Judson had a very strong relish for litera-

---

[1] About $2,600   [2] About $1,000.

ture and linguistic research.   One cannot fail to observe
the poetic gems, original and quoted, scattered through
his correspondence.   The Burman literature, with its
Buddhistic books and its fascinating poetry, was a vast
mine unexplored.   He was tempted to trace the winding
paths which were ever opening before his scholarly mind,
and to search this great and ancient treasure-vault.
Might he not translate into English some beautiful fragments of this literature, and so enkindle in some of the
highly organized minds of the Western world a greater
interest in foreign missions?   But no.   He turned reso-
lutely away from the alluring prospect.   He was determined not to know anything among the Burmans save
Jesus Christ and him crucified.   As a missionary he was
unwilling to disperse his mental forces over the wide surface of literary and philosophical pursuits, but insisted on
moving along the narrow and divinely appointed groove
of unfolding the word of God and meting it out to suit
the wants of perishing man.

But perhaps the severest sacrifice of all was the denial
of his social instincts.   It was not because he was unen-
dowed with social sensibilities that he so cut himself off
from the State or conventional dinner, and from a fashion-
able intercourse with Sir Archibald Campbell, and other
cultivated Englishmen, as to incur the stigma of being
called "odd."   He did not withdraw to his hermitage in
the jungle because he was a fierce and sullen fanatic.   On
the contrary, one who knew him most intimately says
that "Perhaps his most remarkable characteristic to a
superficial observer was the extent and thorough genial
nature of his sociableness."   Indeed, there was a spice
of truth in the remark sneeringly made by a fashion-
able woman that "Judson abstained from society not from

principle, but from cowardice—he was like the drunkard who was afraid to taste lest he should not know when to stop." "His ready humor," Mrs. Judson writes, "his aptness at illustration, his free flow of generous, gentlemanly feeling made his conversation peculiarly brilliant and attractive, and such interchanges of thought and feeling were his delight." "He was not," she adds, "a born angel, shut without the pale of humanity by his religion." His was not the stern, unæsthetic nature of the great Reformer and theologian who, though he lived his life on the lake of Geneva, nowhere betrays in his voluminous writings that he was at all conscious of the beautiful panorama spread out before him. He was, as has been said of another, "a creature who entered into every one's feelings, and could take the pressure of their thought instead of urging his own with iron resistance." He was, in truth,

> . . . Not too bright or good
> For human nature's daily food;
> For transient sorrows, simple wiles,
> Praise, blame, love, kisses, tears, and smiles.

The author, among his own scanty childhood recollections of his father, well remembers the tenderness with which he nursed his sick boy; and a missionary associate says: "He had a peculiarly fascinating way of endearing himself to everybody whose hearts were open to his kindness." Mrs. E. C. Judson writes:

"He was always planning pleasant little surprises for family and neighbors, and kept up through his married life those little lover-like attentions which I believe husbands are apt to forget. There was, and always must have been, a kind of *romance* about him (you will understand I use the word italicized for want of a better), which prevented every-day life with him from ever being common-place. If he went out before I was awake in the morning, very likely some pretty message would be pinned to my mosquito curtain. If he was obliged to stay at a business meeting or any such place longer than he thought I expected, and often when he did not stay over the time, some little penciled line that he could trace without attracting attention, would be dispatched to me. And often when he sat at his study table, something droll or tender or encouraging or suggestive of thought, penciled on a broken scrap of paper, sometimes the margin of a newspaper, was every little while finding its way to my room. . . He was always earnest, enthusiastic, sympathizing even in the smallest trifles, tender, delicate, and considerate—never moody, as he has sometimes been described, but equally communicative, whether sad or cheerful. . . He was always, even in his playfulness, intellectual; and the more familiar, the more elevated."

The little thoughtful attentions which he was continually paying to his fellow-missionaries, betrayed with what heartiness he entered into all their joys and sorrows. His friends, the Bennetts, had sent their children to America. One day Mr. Judson surprised them with a present of the portraits of their absent little ones, for which he had himself sent to this country.

He had a remarkable gift for comforting people, and was indeed a son of consolation. A lady to whom he paid a visit of condolence upon the death of her mother wrote to her friend: "He must have been peculiarly sympathetic himself, or he could not have entered into every one's sorrows so easily." If any one was in trouble, he was sure to be there. Every tone of his voice seemed calculated to touch the innermost chord of a troubled heart.

We left Mr. Judson, when we turned aside to look at his character, by the freshly made graves of his wife and child at Amherst. Amherst and Moulmein, situated about twenty-five miles apart upon the coast of a newly settled province, were competing for the honor of being the metropolis of British Burma. They were both planted in the jungle, dependent for their growth upon the tide of population which kept streaming away from the oppressions of Burman despotism toward the enlightened and liberal English rule that prevailed throughout the Tenasserim provinces. The scale, as has already been stated, was turned in favor of Moulmein, by the fact that Sir Archibald Campbell had chosen it as the headquarters of his army. It consequently grew into a large city with marvelous rapidity, while Amherst dwindled into insignificance.

The missionaries at first thought it best to have two stations, one at Amherst and the other at Moulmein—the Wades to hold the ground in the former place, and the Boardmans in the latter, while Mr. Judson should move backward and forward between the two points. But they soon decided not to attempt to keep their hold on Amherst, but to concentrate all their forces in Moulmein. This town, as has been said, was situated at the mouth of the Salwen, on its west bank. It consisted principally of one street which extended along the river front about two miles. Behind the city was a long range of hills, dotted here and there with the graceful pagoda. In front swept the broad swift Salwen, "in which an English sloop-of-war was lying at anchor, and curiously shaped Indian boats were passing to and fro with each changing tide." Directly across the river lay the province of Martaban, still under Burman rule, the secure haunt of robbers and pirates; while far off to the seaward one could catch a glimpse of the high hills of Ballou Island.

The Boardmans were the first to remove to Moulmein, and were soon followed by the Wades, while Mr. Judson came last. We find in Mr. Boardman's journal, under date of August 12, 1827, the following minute:

"The Bufman merchant to whom I gave the books called on me yesterday for further information on some point which he did not fully understand. While he was here the head man of the village also came; and these two together, with our Burman teacher, who seems to be inquiring, entered into some particular discussion of Christian history and doctrine. In the midst of this discussion, how great was my joy on beholding Mr. Judson approaching the house. It is now probable that we shall all be settled together at this place."

The mission house had been erected by the Boardmans at the expense of the mission, upon ground given by Sir Archibald Campbell. It was situated about a mile south of the English barracks, on a gentle westerly and southerly declivity, so that it commanded a view of the river and the sea. It contained three rooms fifteen feet square, and a veranda on all sides, but enclosed on three sides for a study, store room, dressing room, etc. The general had offered the missionaries a site within the cantonments, but they chose rather to be where they could come into closer and more direct contact with the natives. This, however, exposed them landward to tigers, and riverward to robbers from Martaban.

It was at this exposed spot that the Judsons, the Boardmans, and the Wades mustered their forces, and stood prepared to take advantage of the inflowing tide

of Burmese population. They took with them from
Amherst their whole little flock of native converts and
inquirers, namely, Moung Shwa-ba, Moung Ing, Moung
Myat-poo, Mah Doke, with her husband, Moung Dwah,
and Ko Thah-byu, who afterward became the apostle
to the Karens. Seventeen of the female scholars also
accompanied them, besides the two little boys left motherless by the lamented Mah Men-la.

The missionaries and their converts at once began *zayat*
work. There were soon in Moulmein four widely separated centers of gospel influence, namely: The mission
house where Mr. Boardman labored; Mr. Judson's *zayat*,
about two miles and a half north of the mission premises,
in a very populous part of the town (" a little shed project-
ing into one of the dirtiest, noisiest streets of the place ");
Mr. Wade's *zayat*, out in the country, about half a mile
south of the mission house; and, besides, a reading *zayat*,
where Moung Shwa-ba and Moung Ing alternately read
the Scriptures to all the passers-by. At each of these
stations public worship was held, followed by close personal conversation with any who desired to become
acquainted with the new religion. Nor did the word
thus preached return void. They soon had the happiness of baptizing Moung Dwah, one of the inquirers who
had accompanied them from Amherst, and others speedily
followed his example.

But not only was the *zayat work* crowned with success,
the *school work* was not less effective. The school of girls
which had been transplanted from Amherst increased in
size and efficiency under the superintendence of Mrs. Wade
and Mrs. Boardman, who not only taught the children,
but imparted religious instruction to the Burman women.
The tireless Boardman also opened a school for boys.

Mr. Judson speaks joyously of an incipient revival in the girls' school, "similar to those glorious revivals which distinguish our own beloved land."

But amid the cares and toils of beginning a missionary enterprise in Moulmein, Mr. Judson did not remit his literary labors. The odd moments of time left from zayat work and school work were filled with the work of translation. Even before leaving Amherst he had embarked upon the prodigious task of translating the Old Testament into Burmese. He had begun with the Psalms. After the death of his wife and child his sorrowing heart instinctively turned for consolation to "the prayers of David, the son of Jesse."

While thus absorbed in the work of preaching and teaching and translating at Moulmein, he was not forgetful of the smouldering campfires he had left behind him at Rangoon and Amherst. At Rangoon especially, where he had first unfurled the banner of the Christ, and whence he had been rudely driven by the intolerant spirit of the king of Ava, a native church was speedily reorganized under a Burman pastor, Ko Thah-a, one of the original Rangoon converts.

Ko Thah-a visited Mr. Judson at Moulmein in order to be instructed as to what he should do with those whom he had persuaded to accept of Christ, and who wished to be baptized. It was thought best to ordain him as pastor of the church in Rangoon.

What a stubborn vitality there is in that seminal divine idea—a local church. Mr. and Mrs. Judson formed such a church, when in 1813 they made their home at the mouth of the Irawadi, and all by themselves shared in that Holy Supper which was instituted to commemorate the Saviour's dying love. The church of two slowly grew into a church of twenty. Then came the war, and the long imprisonment of the pastor at Ava. The church was hewed to the ground. Only four members could be found, and these were transplanted to Amherst. More than two years later Ko Thah-a, who had been lost sight of in the interior of the country, makes his appearance in Moulmein. He has all along been secretly preaching the good news, and now he wants to go back to Rangoon and baptize the converts whom he has won. Out of the stump of the tree cut down there springs a shoot which has bloomed and flourished even to the present time. The Rangoon mission of 1892 embraces eighty-six churches, and four thousand five hundred and sixty-nine members. "There shall be a handful of corn in the earth upon the top of the mountains; the fruit thereof shall shake like Lebanon."

Ko Thah-a, the first Christian pastor among the Burmans, proved to be an able minister. Again and again he sent to Moulmein the cheering news of conversions and baptisms; and when, a year and a half after his ordination, Mr. Judson visited him at Rangoon and invited him to go on a missionary tour up the country, he declined, " on account of having so many irons in the fire "—that is, hopeful inquirers—that he must stay to bring forward and baptize. And Mr. Judson adds, "He is as solicitious and busy as a hen pressing about her chickens. It is quite refreshing to hear him talk on the subject, and see what a nice, careful old shepherd he makes. The Lord bless his soul and the souls of his flock! "

Neither did Mr. Judson forget the deserted mission field at Amherst, where lay the precious dust of his wife and child. Like the Apostle Paul, he felt the deepest solicitude for the spiritual welfare of the converts whom he had left along the track behind him. Moung Ing was ordained and sent to be pastor of the disciples at Amherst.

Moung Ing, however, though diligent and faithful and extremely desirous of doing good, seems to have proved rather a failure as a minister. The prospects at Amherst darkened. One feels his heart drawn out toward the poor fisherman, Moung Ing, one of the very earliest Burman converts, Mrs. Judson's only dependence at Ava and Oung-pen-la—the first bearer of the gospel to the Tavoyans, and yet a man whose mission in this world, in spite of zeal, fidelity, and untiring industry, seemed to be ever to fail.

But the time had now come when this little company of missionaries at Moulmein had to be broken up. Judson, Boardman, and Wade—an illustrious triumvirate—could not long expect to work together in the same place. This would be too great a concentration of forces at one point. The gospel light must be more widely dispersed through the thick gloom of paganism. The Boardmans were the first to go, though the parting with their missionary associates was attended with the keenest suffering. Besides, they had originated the mission at Moulmein, and it was at a peculiar sacrifice that they pressed into the regions beyond. They chose Tavoy as their field of work. It seemed out of the question to assail Burma proper; and on the long coast of the ceded provinces, Amherst having dwindled into insignificance, Tavoy was the only important point within a hundred and fifty miles. If they went to Arracan, British territory situated on the other side of Burma proper, they would be too far away to meet with the other missionaries for such occasional consultation and concert of prayer as seemed advisable to the Board at home. Accordingly, on the 29th of March, 1828, when the missionaries had experienced for only seven months the joy of laboring together in Moulmein, Mr. and Mrs. Boardman, with their little family, set sail for Tavoy. They were accompanied by a young Siamese convert, Moung Shway-pwen, by a Karen, Ko Thah-byu—subsequently the renowned apostle to the Karens—and by four of the native schoolboys. With this little group of disciples, Mr. Boardman began that brief and heroic campaign among the Karens which has made his name so illustrious in the annals of missions.

On the 15th of December, 1829, Mr. Judson received news of the death at Washington of his brother Elnathan, with whom he had prayed so many years before by the roadside on his way from Plymouth to Boston. The letter that brought him these sad tidings assured him also that the wayside prayer had been answered.

On the arrival at Moulmein of two new missionaries, the printer, Mr. Cephas Bennett, and his wife, it seemed best that the policy of dispersion should be still more rigorously pursued. Mr. Judson never approved of the concentration of missionaries at any one station.

He believed in multiplying the centers of light. It might be well for a new missionary upon his first arrival to be kept in training at some long-established post in association with experienced laborers, but then his ultimate aim should be to plunge alone into the thickest of heathenism.

Besides, the time had now come to make a new attempt to enter Burma proper. Accordingly, on February 21, 1830, Mr. and Mrs. Wade removed to Rangoon, Mr. Judson's old field, where the newly ordained Moung

Thah-a and Moung Ing were laboring. The pain of parting was alleviated by the hope which Mr. Judson cherished of joining them again at Rangoon, with the purpose of once more penetrating the valley of the Ira-wadi in the direction of Ava.

He could not remain content at Moulmein. He was not satisfied with founding two or three missions on the outermost edge of British Burma. He longed to penetrate Burma proper again, and establish a line of mission stations in the Irawadi valley, that arterial channel through which the tide of Burmese population surged. Mr. Wade had gone before simply as an *avant-coureur*. His going to Rangoon was only a part of a more general movement. Leaving Moulmein in charge of Mr. Boardman, who had been temporarily recalled from Tavoy, Mr. Judson parted with him and the new-comers, Mr. and Mrs. Bennett, on April 26, 1830, and set sail for Rangoon, where he arrived six days later.

He spent only a few days with Mr. Wade in Rangoon. Then, in the company of five native disciples, he proceeded by boat to Prome, an ancient city situated on the Irawadi about one hundred and seventy miles from the mouth.

This brave effort, however, to plant Christianity at Prome, in the very interior of the Burman empire, the half-way place between Rangoon and Ava, proved a complete failure. Mr. Judson preached the gospel and distributed tracts all the way up the river, and for three months he and his disciples labored faithfully in Prome. He occupied daily an old tumbledown *zayat* at the foot of the great pagoda, Shway Landau, and thousands heard the gospel from his lips. But suddenly the *zayat* was deserted. He met with cold and rude treatment in the streets. The dogs were allowed to bark at him unmolested. It was rumored that the king at Ava was displeased that the Burman religion should be assailed in the very heart of his empire, and that he had given orders that Mr. Judson should be required to depart from Burma. It subsequently transpired that the king himself was in reality kindly disposed toward Mr. Judson. He had inquired some time before where Mr. Judson was, and when told that he was in Moulmein, he said: "Why does he not come here? He is a good man, and would, if he were here, teach and discipline my ministers and make better men of them." The ejection of Mr. Judson from Burma was a trick on the part of these very prime ministers. They hated all foreign intrusion, and represented to Major Burney, the English ambassador at Ava, that the king was very much displeased with Mr. Judson's attempt to introduce Christianity into the empire.

And so Mr. Judson was forced sadly and reluctantly to abandon his project of carrying the gospel into Central Burma. Although he was foiled in this effort, yet he did not withdraw immediately to Moulmein, but remained for almost a year laboring at Rangoon, situated just within the gate of the empire. He retreated only step by step from before Burman intolerance, disputing every inch of the ground.

Just at this time the whole land seemed peculiarly pervaded by a spirit of religious thirst. Everybody was curious to know about this new religion. The people seemed to catch eagerly at every scrap of information relating to Christianity. The ears of the heathen, to use their own vivid expression, had become *thinner*. Mr. Judson's house was thronged with inquirers. While he was not permitted in person to preach in the interior of the country, yet in Rangoon he freely distributed tracts and translations of the Scriptures, which sped on their way far up the Irawadi toward Ava. He thought it wise to take advantage of this floodtide of eager curiosity. A nation has its moods as well as an individual. Wasteful indolence might indeed substitute the lavish and indiscriminate use of printer's ink for the personal preaching of the gospel by the living voice. But, carefully watching the pulse of Burman life, he believed that at last the time had come when the printed page might be made a mighty engine for good, and could not be too freely used. Hence, to Mr. Bennett, the printer, and to the other missionaries at Moulmein, he sent agonizing appeals for more tracts, the echoes of which were wafted even to our own land.

And while thus striving to satisfy the thirst of the Burmans for religious knowledge, he did not intermit his long and laborious task of translating the Scriptures. He shut himself up in the garret of the mission-house, leaving his Burman associates to deal with the inquirers below, only referring to him the more important cases. In his seclusion he made such long strides in his work that, at the close of his stay at Rangoon, he wrote in his journal: "1831, July 19. Finished the translation of Genesis, twenty chapters of Exodus, Psalms, Solomon's Song, Isaiah, and Daniel."

It was about this time that the Mission Board in this country sent him an earnest and affectionate invitation to revisit his native land. He was about forty-two years old, and had been absent from America eighteen years. His health was shattered. His family he had laid in the grave. He said several years later that he had never seen a ship sail out of the port of Moulmein bound for

England or America without an almost irrepressible inclination to get on board and visit again the home of his boyhood. And yet in reply to this urgent invitation from his brethren, he wrote that he would "not feel justified in accepting their invitation to return home."

While in Rangoon he received the heavy tidings that the beloved Boardman had died in the jungles back of Tavoy. Sorrow had come upon the Boardman family in quick and uninterrupted succession. The death of a little daughter, Sarah, was followed by the revolt of Tavoy, and during this brief uprising of the Burmans against their masters, Mr. Boardman had been subjected to an exposure and hardship such as his consumptive habit was ill able to endure. From that time he visibly declined. To use Mrs. E. C. Judson's words: "His cheeks were a little more hollow, and the color on them more flickering; his eyes were brighter, and seemingly more deeply set beneath the brow, and immediately below them was a faint, indistinct arc of mingled ash and purple like the shadow of a faded leaf; his lips were sometimes of a clayey pallor, and sometimes they glowed with crimson; and his fingers were long, and the hands of a partially transparent thinness."

The newly appointed missionary to the Karens, Mr. Mason, arrived in Tavoy June 3, 1831. "On the jetty," he wrote, "reclining helplessly in the chair which had served the purpose of a carriage, a pale, worn-out man, with the characters of death in his countenance, waited to welcome his successor." Mr. Boardman was preparing to take a tour into the jungle in order to baptize some recent Karen converts. His emaciated form was to be carried on a litter several days' journey into the wilderness. Remonstrance was unvailing; for he had set his

heart upon accomplishing his purpose. Besides, it was
thought that the change of air might do him good.
Even after setting out, he was advised to return; but his
reply was: "The cause of God is of more importance
than my health, and if I return now, our whole object
will be defeated. I want to see the work of the Lord go
on."

After a long journey of several days through the
wilderness, he witnessed the baptism of thirty-four
Karens, and died in the heart of the jungle sustained by
the presence of the native disciples, his infant son, and
devoted wife, who in describing the scene writes as
follows:

> With the love-light in his eyes,
> Mute the dying teacher lies.
> It is finished. Bear him back!
> Haste along the jungle track!
> See the lid uplifting now—
> See the glory on his brow.
>
> It is finished. Wood and glen
> Sigh their mournful, meek Amen.
> 'Mid that circle, sorrow spanned,
> Clasping close an icy hand,
> Lo! the midnight watcher wan,
> Waiting yet another dawn.

When Mrs. Boardman with her son George, about two
years and a half old, were thus suddenly left in all the
perplexity and desolation of widowhood and fatherless-
ness, she received from Mr. Judson the following words of
tenderest consolation and counsel:

"RANGOON, March 4, 1831.

"MY DEAR SISTER:—You are now drinking the
bitter cup whose dregs I am somewhat acquainted with.

And though, for some time, you have been aware of its approach, I venture to say that it is far bitterer than you expected. It is common for persons in your situation to refuse all consolation, to cling to the dead, and to fear that they shall too soon forget the dear object of their affections. But don't be concerned. I can assure you that months and months of heartrending anguish are before you, whether you will or not. I can only advise you to take the cup with both hands, and sit down quietly to the bitter repast which God has appointed for your sanctification. As to your beloved, you *know* that all his tears are wiped away, and that the diadem which encircles his brow outshines the sun. Little Sarah and the other have again found their father; not the frail, sinful mortal that they left the earth, but an immortal saint, a magnificent, majestic king. What more can you desire for them? While therefore your tears flow, let a due proportion be tears of joy. Yet take the bitter cup with both hands, and sit down to your repast. You will soon learn a secret, that there is sweetness at the bottom. You will find the sweetest cup that you ever tasted in all your life. You will find heaven coming near to you, and familiarity with your husband's voice will be a connecting link, drawing you almost within the sphere of celestial music."

CHAPTER X

LIFE IN MOULMEIN (*Continued*). 1831-1845

IT now became Mr. Judson's duty to return to Moulmein. He had been absent thirteen months. The first part of that time had been spent in the futile effort to establish a mission at Prome, and during the last part he had labored alone with native converts at Rangoon, distributing tracts, preaching the gospel, and translating the Scriptures. Mr. and Mrs. Wade had repaired to Rangoon soon after his return from Prome; but Mrs. Wade's health had so completely broken that it was thought best for her and her husband to take a voyage to America. The ship in which the Wades sailed was driven out of its course by violent gales, and at last put into a port on the coast of Arracan. Here Mrs. Wade's health was so much improved that the idea of going to America was given up, and they returned to Moulmein instead. But, in the meantime, Mr. Judson's presence seemed indispensable there. A new party of missionaries had arrived from America, including Mr. and Mrs. Mason, Mr. and Mrs. Kincaid, and Mr. and Mrs. Jones. The Masons had gone to Tavoy, Mr. Jones went to Rangoon to take Mr. Judson's place, and the Kincaids were still staying at Moulmein.

When he returned to Moulmein he saw much to delight his heart. The little church had been enlarged by the baptism of many Burmese, Karens, and Talings. Two million pages of tracts and translations of Scriptures had

130

been printed. The missionaries had also made repeated journeys into the jungle, where a church of fourteen members had been organized at a place called Wades-ville, in honor of the missionary who had first preached the gospel there. At the close of 1831, Mr. Judson reported, on behalf of the Burman mission, two hundred and seventeen persons as baptized during the year ; one hundred and thirty-six at Moulmein, seventy-six at Tavoy, and five at Rangoon.

Soon after returning from Rangoon to Moulmein he entered upon a new field of operations. Whenever his close confinement to the work of translation necessitated a change of air and scene, it was his custom to take a tour among the wild Karen tribes occupying the jungle back of Moulmein. His restless spirit was always long-ing to press into the interior of the country, and the great Irawadi valley being closed to him, there was nothing left but to penetrate Burma by the Salwen and its tribu-taries, which constitute the second of the river systems by which the land is drained.

The Karens, as their very name indicates, were wild men. They are distributed throughout Burma, Siam, and parts of China, and number from two hundred to four hundred thousand. They are perhaps the remnant of an aboriginal and subjugated race, and are looked down upon by the Burmese as inferiors. They speak a different lan-guage, and have distinct race characteristics. They are peculiarly accessible to the Christian religion, being de-void of the pride and dogmatism which characterize the Burmans. Besides they had a hoary tradition that white messengers would come from the sea to teach them.

While the Burmans lived in towns and cities, the Karens, like our Indians, occupied villages far back in the jungle, by the side of mountain streams. Mr. Judson's attention was first called to them in Rangoon. "They formed small parties of strange, wild-looking men, clad in unshapely garments, who from time to time straggled past his residence." He was told that they were as untamable as the wild cow of the mountains; that they seldom entered a town except on compulsion, and were nomadic in their habits. A British officer gives a singular instance of their wildness:

"An officer was lying on his bed in a little room inside the stockaded police post, which had a narrow gate with an armed sentry on guard; the hillman, with the minimum of clothing, was introduced by a smart sergeant, who coaxed him to approach. He cautiously and distrustfully, and with great persuasion, advanced stooping to the bed; when close to it he gave one long, steady look at the white man; suddenly, with a yell, threw himself up straight, turned round, dashed out of the room, through the gate, upsetting the armed sentry, rushed across a little stream at the bottom of the stockade, and, clambering like a monkey sheer up the side of the opposite mountain, never stopped till he was lost to sight in the forest."

In order to secure permanent churches among the Karens, the first step of the missionaries was to persuade them to settle down in one place and form large and well-ordered villages. It was in this way that the town of Wadesville, before mentioned, sprang into existence. Christianity has thus proved a powerful agent in civilizing the Karens, and a Christian village is easily distinguished from a heathen one, not only by its size, but by its cleanly and regular streets.

Mr. Judson's tours in the Karen jungles were attended with great fatigue and danger. He was always accom-

panied by a band of associates. He would take
him eight or ten disciples, and dispatch them right
left up the tributaries of the Salwen. Two by two th\
would penetrate the wilderness, and meeting their teacher
a few days later, would report to him the results of their
labor. The Oriental, under good leadership, makes a
faithful and intrepid follower. And Mr. Judson's magnetism of character held his assistants to him with hooks
of steel. He had the gift of getting work, and their best
work, out of the converted natives. Promising boys and
young men he took under his own instruction, and qualified them to become teachers and ministers.

At the close of the year 1832 Mr. Judson reported one
hundred and forty-three baptisms; three at Rangoon,
seventy at Moulmein, sixty-seven at Tavoy, and three at
Mergui. This made five hundred and sixteen who had
been baptized since his arrival in Burma, only seventeen
of whom had been finally excluded.

But the time had at last come when Mr. Judson's long
domestic solitude was to end. Under date of April 10,
1834, we find in his journal the following important
entry:

"Was married to Mrs. Sarah H. Boardman, who was
born at Alstead, New Hampshire, November 4, 1803, the
eldest daughter of Ralph and Abiah O. Hall—married
to George D. Boardman, July 4, 1825—left a widow
February 11, 1831, with one surviving child, George D.
Boardman, born August 18, 1828."

Nearly eight years of loneliness had passed since he
laid his beloved Ann beneath the hopia-tree. He had
arrived at the age of forty-six when he married Mrs.
Boardman. He found in her a kindred spirit. She had
spent the three years of widowhood in heroic toil among

the Karens at Tavoy, and had turned persistently away
from the urgent appeals of her friends in America to
return home for her own sake and the sake of her little
boy. For three years this beautiful and intrepid woman
continued her husband's work. She was the guiding
spirit of the mission. She pointed out the way of life to
the Karen inquirers who came in from the wilderness.
She conducted her schools with such tact and ability that
when, afterward, an appropriation was obtained from the
English Government for schools throughout the provinces,
it was expressly stipulated that they should be " conducted
on the plan of Mrs. Boardman's schools at Tavoy." She
even made long missionary tours into the Karen jungles.
With her little boy carried by her followers at her side,
she climbed the mountains, traversed the marshes, forded
the streams, and threaded the forests. On one of these
trips she sent back a characteristic message to Mrs. Mason
at Tavoy: " Perhaps you had better send the chair, as it
is convenient to be carried over the streams when they
are deep. You will laugh when I tell you that I have
forded all the smaller ones."

Soon after their marriage, Mr. and Mrs. Judson were
compelled to part with little George Boardman. He was
but six years old, and yet had reached an age when a
child begins to be, in a peculiar sense, the companion of
parents. But the children of Anglo-Saxon residents in
the East have to be sent home at an early age, otherwise
they are in danger of death under the debilitating influence of the Oriental climate; or if they get their growth
at all, are liable to feebleness of mind and body. Such a
separation between parent and child cannot but be peculiarly distressing to the missionary. He devotes himself
for life and expects to die on the field, and thus the part-

ing bids fair to be final. Other Europeans and Americans are merely temporary residents in the East, and though also compelled to send their children home, may reasonably hope to meet them once more after a short separation. The missionary's child, on the other hand, must be permanently consigned to the care of distant strangers. This is, perhaps, the keenest suffering that falls to the lot of a missionary.

It was a heavy day for Mrs. Judson when her husband carried to the ship "Cashmere" the child[1] who had been the sharer of all her sufferings and griefs at Tavoy. It was well for her that a veil hid from her eyes the immediate future, else she might have seen the boy's hairbreadth escape from pirates and the tortures of mind to which the shrinking child was subjected on board the ship which was bearing him away from his mother's side.

While in Moulmein, Mr. Judson completed the Burman Bible. It was about the time of his marriage to Mrs. Boardman that he finished the first rough draft. Seventeen years before in Rangoon, all he had to offer of the precious Scriptures to the first Burman inquirer was two half-sheets containing the first five chapters of Matthew. From that time on, beneath all his toils and sufferings and afflictions, there moved the steady undercurrent of this great purpose and labor of Bible translation. It was a task for which he had little relish. He much preferred dealing with the Burmans individually, and persuading them one by one of the truth of the gospel. In a letter which states his purpose of relinquishing for many months the pleasure of laboring in the

---

[1] George Dana Boardman, D. D., LL. D., Pastor Emeritus of the First Baptist Church, Philadelphia.

Karen jungles in order to shut himself up to the work of translation, he says: "The tears flow as I write." Alluding to this same labor of translation, he writes to the corresponding secretary: "And so, God willing and giving us life and strength, we hope to go on, but we hope still to be allowed to feel that our great work is to preach the gospel *viva voce*, and build up the glorious kingdom of Christ among this people."

But the translation of the Bible was essentially neccssary to the permanent establishment of Christianity in Burma, and no other living man was qualified for the work. And so, in the brief intervals of preaching and teaching and imprisonment and jungle travel, secluding himself in the garret at Rangoon and afterward in the little room attached to the mission-house at Moulmein, he quietly wrought at this prodigious task until, at last, he could write on January 31, 1834, at the age of fifty-six:

"Thanks be to God, I can *now* say I have attained. I have knelt down before him with the last leaf in my hand, and imploring his forgiveness for all the sins which have polluted my labors in this department, and his aid in future efforts to remove the errors and imperfections which necessarily cleave to the work, I have commended it to his mercy and grace; I have dedicated it to his glory. May he make his own inspired word, now complete in the Burman tongue, the grand instrument of filling all Burma with songs of praise to our great God and Saviour Jesus Christ. Amen."

Great as was the task of thus scrupulously translating the Bible, the revision was still more laborious. Seven years were spent in revising the first work. It was a mental peculiarity of Mr. Judson never to leave a thing alone while it could possibly be improved. His besetting sin was, in his own expressive words alluded to before, a *lust for finishing,* and it was not until October, 1840, that he could say:

" On the 24th of October last I enjoyed the great happiness of committing to the press the last sheet of the new edition of the Burmese Bible."

In regard to its merits his estimate was very modest. He says:

" I never read a chapter without pencil in hand, and Griesbach and Parkhurst at my elbow; and it will be an object to me through life to bring the translation to such a state that it may be a standard work."

How far his own humble view falls short of doing justice to the excellence of his monumental task, may be gathered from the following statement by President Francis Wayland:

" Competent judges affirm that Dr. Judson's translation of the Scriptures is the most perfect work of the kind that has yet appeared in India. On this subject it will not be inappropriate to introduce a few sentences from the pen of a gentleman high in rank in India, himself a distinguished linguist and a proficient in the Burmese language: 'The best judges pronounce it to be all that he aimed at making it; and also, what with him never was an object, an imperishable monument of the man's genius. We may venture to hazard the opinion that as Luther's Bible is now in the hands of Protestant Germany, so three centuries hence, Judson's Bible will be the Bible of the Christian churches of Burma.' "

From this point our narrative naturally assumes a more domestic character; and we are permitted to see

Mr. Judson's deep tenderness as a husband and a father.
Some of the greatest objects of his life having been
achieved, and his health beginning to decline, his restless
spirit turned instinctively to family life for repose. On
October 31, 1835, his heart was cheered by the birth of a
daughter, whose name, Abby Ann, associates her with
his only sister, from whom he had parted so many years
before, and also with her whom he left sleeping beneath
the hopia-tree.

A son was born April 7, 1837, Adoniram Brown
Judson, who was soon followed by his little brother,
Elnathan. But Mr. Judson's iron purposes were not
melted in the ease and quiet of home life. He did not
cease his efforts to save his poor Burmans. A few weeks
after the birth of his son, he wrote :

"My days are commonly spent in the following
manner : the morning in reading Burman ; the forenoon
in a public *zayat* with some assistant, preaching to those
who call ; the afternoon in preparing or revising something for the press, correcting proof-sheets, etc. ; the evening in conducting worship in the native chapel, and con-
versing with the assistants or other native Christians or
inquirers."

Upon the completion of the fiftieth year of his life, and of
his twenty-fifth year in Burma, it is not strange that even
his wiry physique should have begun to give way beneath
the strain. Disease fastened first upon his lungs, entailing
loss of voice and intense pain. It was thought that a
short voyage to Calcutta would restore his health. He
set sail on February 19, 1839, and after an absence of
nearly two months, during which he had a delightful visit
with the English Baptists of Calcutta and Serampore, he
returned to Moulmein, his health somewhat improved.

The sadness of this separation from the faithful wife and mother, whom he left behind at Moulmein, was intensified by the apprehension that he might die on the voyage.

The native Christians at Moulmein were glad enough, after an interval of ten months, to hear again the voice of their beloved teacher, though he still spoke in feeble accents, and was far from convalescence. In a letter to a fellow-missionary he refers playfully to the birth of another son at the close of 1839: "Master Henry came into notice the last day of the year; but there was no earthquake or anything."

Mrs. Judson's health also began to fail. She was attacked by the disease which finally terminated her life at St. Helena. The children too were all sick, so that a sea voyage was needed for the very preservation of the family. Mr. Judson reluctantly decided to embark with his wife and four children for Calcutta.

"We had been out only four days," says Mrs. Judson, in speaking of this voyage, "when we struck on shoals, and for about twenty minutes were expecting to see the large, beautiful vessel a wreck; and then all on board must perish, or at best take refuge in a small boat, exposed to the dreary tempest. I shall never forget my feelings, as I looked over the side of the vessel that night on the dark ocean, and fancied ourselves, with our poor, sick, and almost dying children, launched on its stormy waves. The captain tacked as soon as possible, and the tide rising at the time, we were providentially delivered from our extreme peril."

When the family arrived at Serampore, just above Calcutta, they hired "a nice, dry house on the very bank of the river." But, though the sea air had naturally revived the invalids, as soon as they came fairly under the

hot climate of Bengal they all suffered a relapse. What
was to be done? They met at Calcutta a pious Scotch
sea captain, whose vessel was going to the Isle of France,
and from thence to Moulmein. He made the kind pro-
posal to take the whole family on such terms that this
circuitous course would cost them no more than to go
directly to Moulmein. They dreaded the voyage in the
month of August, which is a very dangerous month in
the bay of Bengal, but there seemed to be no other
alternative. So Mr. Judson accordingly accepted Captain Hamlin's offer, and decided to set sail for that island
to which he had repaired nearly thirty years before, when
he had been driven from Bengal by the East India Company. But before leaving Serampore the fond parents
were compelled to bury their little Henry, at the age of
one year and seven months.

Bidding farewell to his newly made grave, Mr. and
Mrs. Judson, with their sick children, embarked on board
the "Ramsay." The voyage to the Isle of France occupied
about six weeks, and as the monsoon was drawing to a
close, the storms were very frequent, sudden, and severe.
Mrs. Judson thus records their experience:

"Could you now look on our dismasted vessel you
would indeed say, she is a 'ship in distress.' For the last
three days we have had the most frightful squalls I ever
experienced; and yesterday two topmasts, a top-gallant
mast, and the jib-boom, with all their sails, were torn
away, causing a tremendous crash. For the last two
nights I have not closed my eyes to sleep, and I find it
quite impossible to sleep now. I have, therefore, taken
my pen, though the vessel rolls so that I fear my writing
will be quite illegible. Do not infer from anything I
have said that I am suffering from terror; my wakeful-

ness has been occasioned only by bodily discomfort, aris-
ing from the violent tossing of the vessel. I thank God
that I feel perfectly calm and resigned; and I can leave
myself and my dear family in his hands, with a feeling
of perfect peace and composure."

But the voyage, severe as it was, proved very beneficial
to the invalids, and, after spending a month in Port Louis,
they returned to Moulmein, where they arrived on December 10, in greatly improved health. Captain Hamlin
declined to receive any compensation for the passage from
Calcutta to Moulmein *via* the Isle of France, although a
fair charge for the double voyage would have been two
thousand rupees, or about one thousand dollars. The
money which Mr. Judson sent him, merely as an expression of his gratitude, was returned, the noble sailor saying
that he considered it a privilege to have been able to show
some kindness to the servants of Christ. Mr. Judson
wrote at once to the Board, suggesting that it should send
to the captain a formal letter of thanks, together with a
present, "say of a set of the 'Comprehensive Commentary,'" to be addressed to Captain Thomas Hamlin, Jr.,
Greenock, Scotland.

Soon after Mr. and Mrs. Judson and their three children
returned to Moulmein, another son was given them.
He was named Henry, after the little boy whom they had
left in his lonely grave at Serampore.

About this time Mr. Judson heard of the death of his
venerable mother, who departed this life in Plymouth,
Mass., in the eighty-third year of her age. His father
and brother, Elnathan, had died before; and his sister,
Abigail, was now left alone at Plymouth.

At this time also there was pressed upon him a great
task, and one from which he had long shrunk. The

Board at home urgently desired him to undertake the compilation of a Burman dictionary. His heart longed to be engaged in direct individual work, winning souls to Christ. He had no relish for the seclusion which the work of translation required. But no one else seemed qualified for this task, and the failure of his voice imperatively forbade his preaching. And so, with the utmost reluctance, he turned toward a work which was to occupy a large part of his time during the rest of his life.

CHAPTER XI

WHILE thus plodding on in his gigantic task of compiling a Burman dictionary, Mr. Judson found it necessary to embark on a voyage to his native land. Thirty-three years had elapsed since the memorable nineteenth of February, 1812, when he and Mrs. Judson had stood on the deck of the brig "Caravan," and watched the rocky shores of New England fade out of their sight. How swiftly had these years taken their flight,—the one spent in the voyage to Burma, the ten of foundation-laying in Rangoon, the two of suffering in Ava and Oung-pen-la, the two of transition in Amherst, and the eighteen of varied plodding toil in Moulmein. And now the young man of twenty-four had become a veteran of fifty-seven. Again and again he had been invited by the Board to revisit his beloved native land and recruit his wasting forces, but he had steadily declined. More than five years before he had received from the corresponding secretary an urgent invitation to return. Nevertheless the faithful missionary had worked patiently on, refusing to leave his field. At last, however, a return to America became imperative in order to preserve Mrs. Judson's life. After the birth of two children, Charles,[1] born December 18, 1843, and Edward, born December 27, 1844, her health rapidly declined. She had taken several short journeys along the coast without receiving any perma-

---

[1] Died in infancy.

nent benefit. On one of these trips she was accompanied
by her eldest child, Abby, who was about ten years old,
and also by the little invalid Charlie; Mr. Judson with
his four boys, Adoniram, Elnathan, Henry, and the infant
Edward, remaining behind at Moulmein. But as has
already been stated, these short trips along the Tenasserim coast proved quite unavailing, Mrs. Judson's condition was almost desperate, and the only hope of saving
this precious life lay in a voyage to America.

On April 26, 1845, Mr. and Mrs. Judson, with the
three elder children, Abby, Adoniram, and Elnathan,
embarked on the ship "Paragon" bound for London.
They were accompanied by two Burman assistants,
as it was Mr. Judson's purpose to spend a portion of
each day upon the Burman dictionary. The three
younger children, Henry, Charles, and Edward were
left behind in the tender care of the missionaries at Moulmein. The first part of the voyage was so rough that the.
vessel sprang a leak, and the captain determined to put
in at the Isle of France; and on July 5 the ship, with
its precious freight, arrived at Port Louis. Mrs. Judson
had so far improved in health that the two missionaries
formed the purpose of separating, as it was thought that
Mrs. Judson would now be able to continue the voyage
to America alone, while Mr. Judson should return to his
work in Moulmein. It would be hard to find a parallel
for this instance of heroic self-sacrifice. Of these two
returning missionaries, one was a poor, shattered invalid,
consenting to forego her beloved husband's society and to
take the long westward journey in solitude; the other
relinquishing the prospect of again seeing his native land
after an absence of thirty-three years, and leaving the
side of his sick wife the moment his presence seemed no

longer indispensable, that he might resume his labors among the perishing Burmans. It was under these circumstances that Mrs. Judson wrote the pathetic lines which shall be recited for a memorial of her wheresoever **the** gospel shall be preached in the whole world:

We part on this green islet, love,—
  Thou for the eastern main,
I for the setting sun, love,
  O, when to meet again!

My heart is sad for thee, love,
  For lone thy way will be;
And oft thy tears will fall, love,
  For thy children and for me.

The music of thy daughter's voice
  Thou'lt miss for many a year;
And the merry shout of thine elder **boys**
  Thou'lt list in vain to hear.

When we knelt to see our Henry die,
  And heard his last, faint moan,
Each wiped the tear from th' other's eye;
  Now each must weep alone.

My tears fall fast for thee, love;
  How can I say Farewell!
But go; thy God be with thee, love,
  Thy heart's deep grief to quell.

Yet my spirit clings to thine, love;
  Thy soul remains with me,
And oft we'll hold communion sweet
  O'er the dark and distant sea.

And who can paint our mutual joy,
  When, all our wanderings o'er,
We both shall clasp our infants three
  At home, on Burma's shore!

But higher shall our raptures glow,
  On yon celestial plain,
When the loved and parted here below
  Meet ne'er to part again.

Then gird thine armor on, love,
  Nor faint thou by the way,
Till Buddh shall fall, and Burma's sons
  Shall own Messiah's sway.

The two native assistants were therefore sent back to Moulmein, and Mr. Judson expected to follow them as soon as he had seen Mrs. Judson fairly on board ship for America. But she experienced a severe relapse which reduced her strength lower than ever before; and Mr. Judson was soon convinced that it would be impossible for him to leave her, and although he bitterly regretted the loss of his assistants, he felt obliged, after spending three weeks in the Isle of France, to re-embark with Mrs. Judson. They took passage with Captain Codman, of the ship "Sophia Walker," which was bound directly for the United States. On the 25th of July they sailed from Port Louis, and after a time Mrs. Judson appeared to be recovering. But the appearance proved deceptive. There came another relapse which soon terminated in death.

In the cold weather off the Cape of Good Hope she seemed better, but she never really recovered from her last relapse, and though sometimes better, continued on the whole to decline until they neared St. Helena, when all hope of her recovery was given up. She lingered until August 1, when, at three o'clock in the morning, she obtained her release from further suffering, and entered into the joy of her Lord. She was buried in the afternoon of the same day; and in the evening her husband and children were again at sea.

She sleeps sweetly here, on this rock of the ocean,
  · Away from the home of her youth,
And far from the land were, with heartfelt devotion,
  She scattered the bright beams of truth.

The "Sophia Walker," with Mr. Judson and his three children on board, arrived at Boston, October 15, 1845. The missionary who had been so long absent from his native land felt considerable anxiety before going on shore as to where he should secure suitable lodgings in the city. He little dreamed that every home would be thrown open to him, and that soon his progress from city to city would almost assume the proportions of a triumphal march. He was ill prepared for such an enthusiastic greeting. He naturally shrank from observation. He was in exceedingly delicate health. His pulmonary difficulty prevented his speaking much above a husky whisper. He had so long used a foreign tongue that it was hard work for him to form sentences in English. He could address an audience only at second-hand, whispering his words to a speaker at his side, who would convey them to the ears of the hearers. Naturally humble and shy, he found it exceedingly distasteful to be publicly harangued and eulogized. On one occasion, an eye-witness relates that while the returned missionary was listening to words of eloquent praise addressed to him in the presence of a great concourse of people, " his head sank lower and lower until the chin seemed to touch his breast." He wrote to the corresponding secretary: "My chief object in writing is to beg that I may be excused from attending any more such meetings until I get a little better. I expect to be in Boston to-morrow, and shall want two or three days for some necessary business, and propose to go to Worcester on Friday or Saturday; and if I could spend next Sabbath alone in some chamber, I should feel it a great privilege, both as a refreshment to the soul and a relief to the body."

He had come home to find that his native country was

almost a strange land. The railroad system had sprung into existence during his absence. He entered the cars at Worcester one day, and had just taken his seat, when a boy came along with the daily newspapers. He said to Mr. Judson, "Do you want a paper, sir?" "Yes, thank you," the missionary replied, and taking the paper began to read. The newsboy stood waiting for his pay until a lady passenger, occupying the same seat with Mr. Judson, said to him, "The boy expects to be paid for his paper." "Why," replied the missionary, with the utmost surprise, "I have been distributing papers gratuitously in Burma so long that I had no idea the boy was expecting any pay."

He often disappointed public assemblies by declining to relate his own adventures, telling instead the old story of the cross.

His movements in this country were chronicled alike by the secular and religious newspapers. His toils and sufferings had made his name a household word among all Christians, and wherever he went the churches were crowded with people who desired to see and to hear America's pioneer missionary. On the evening of the second day after his arrival a meeting was held in the Bowdoin Square Church, Boston. The following were the closing words of welcome spoken by Dr. Sharp:

"We welcome you to your native land; we welcome you to the scenes of your early and manly youth; we welcome you to our worshiping assemblies; we welcome you to our hearts. As the representative of the ministers and private Christians present, I give to you this hand of cordial welcome, of sympathy, of approbation, and of love. And I believe, could all our denomination be collected in one vast assembly, they would request and empower some one to perform this service for them ; or, rather, each one would prefer to give this significant token of love, and respect, and good wishes, for himself. Were it possible, and could your strength hold out, and your hand bear the grasp and the cordial shake of so many, I could wish that every one who loves the Bible and missions might be his own representative, and give to you, as I do, the hand of an honest, unchanging, and cordial good-will."

And at the close Mr. Judson rose to reply, Dr. Hague standing at his side and interpreting to the multitude these whispered utterances :

"Through the mercy of God I am permitted to stand before you here this evening, a pensioner of your bounty. I desire to thank you for all your sympathy and aid, and I pray God's blessing to rest upon you. . . All that has been done in Burma has been done by the churches, through the feeble and unworthy instrumentality of myself and my brethren. . . It is one of the severest trials of my life not to be able to lift up my voice, and give free utterance to my feelings before this congregation ; but repeated trials have assured me that I cannot safely attempt it. And I am much influenced by the circumstance that it was a request of my wife, in her dying hour, that I would not address public meetings on my arrival. . . I will only add, that I beg your prayers for the brethren I have left in Burma ; for the feeble churches we have planted there ; and that the good work of God's grace may go on until the world shall be filled with his glory."

When he had finished, Dr. Hague continued to address the audience in an eloquent strain until the thread of his address was strangely interrupted. A man had pressed his way through the crowded aisles and had ascended the pulpit. He and Mr. Judson embraced each other with tears of joy and affection. It was Samuel Nott, Jr., the only survivor, except Mr. Judson, of that group of seminary students who had conceived the stupendous idea of American foreign missions. He was one of the five who had first gone to India, but had been compelled to return to America on account of ill health, and now, after a separation of thirty-three years, was permitted to meet his former fellow-student under these circumstances of thrilling interest.

In November, Mr. Judson visited Providence, the seat of Brown University, where he had been graduated about forty years before with the highest honors. A public meeting was held in the old First Baptist Church, which was filled to overflowing. Prayer was offered by Dr. Granger, the pastor of the church, and Dr. Wayland made an address. Mr. Judson then said a few words, which were repeated unto the audience by Dr. Caswell.

The missionary organization which had sustained Mr. Judson in Burma for so many years, opened its triennial convention in New York City, on the 19th of November, 1845. The occasion was one never to be forgotten. Services were held in the Baptist Tabernacle, and Mr. Judson was present. Dr. Cone offered some appropriate resolutions of sympathy and welcome, and then, taking Mr. Judson by the hand, he introduced him to Dr. Wayland, the president of the convention, as Jesus Christ's man.

Mr. Judson, who had been warned by his physicians against speaking in public, could only express his thankfulness in a few simple and touching words. Subse-

quently, in the course of the convention, the proposition
was made to abandon the mission in Arracan. This
brought him to his feet. "Though forbidden to speak
by my medical adviser, I must say a few words. I must
protest against the abandonment of the Arracan mission."
These opening words were audible to all present. Then
his voice sank into a whisper as he stated the reasons why
the mission should not be given up. His closing words
were: "If the convention thinks my services can be dis-
pensed with in finishing my dictionary, I will go immediately to Arracan; or, if God should spare my life to
finish my dictionary, I will go there afterward and labor
there and die and be buried there." It would be impossible to describe the thrilling effect upon the audience of these broken words, uttered in a low whisper,
and reproduced by Dr. Cone. The Arracan mission was
saved.

While Mr. Judson was visiting Bradford, the native
town of his beloved Ann, he learned of the death of
Charlie, one of the little ones whom he had left behind
in Burma.

While on this tour through the country, everywhere
kindling missionary enthusiasm, he met, during a visit in
Philadelphia, Miss Emily Chubbuck, who, under the
nom de plume of Fanny Forester, had achieved a wide
literary reputation, with still wider fame apparently
awaiting her. This lady, who was to take the place at his
side, left successively vacant by Ann Hasseltine and Sarah
Boardman, had been disciplined in the hard school of
poverty. She was born August 22, 1817, at Eaton, a
little town in Central New York, and near a stream
which, with its fringe of alders, murmurs here and there
in her prose and poetry under the name of Alderbrook.

Her parents, Charles Chubbuck and Lavinia Richards, had moved to Eaton from New Hampshire. Her childhood days were spent in a little house on the road from Eaton to West Eaton, perched against a hill so close beneath the road that, as she says, one would feel half disposed "to step from the road where you stood to the top of the chimney." Her parents were very poor, and she thus describes a winter she passed when she was about thirteen years old:

"Father was absent nearly all the time, distributing newspapers; and the severity of the winter so affected his health that he could do but little when he was at home. Mother, Harriet, and I were frequently compelled to go out into the fields, and dig broken wood out of the snow to keep ourselves from freezing. Catherine and I went to the district school as much as we could."

Again she wrote:

"November, 1830. Father's attempt at farming proved, as might have been expected, an entire failure, and for want of a better place he determined to remove to the village. He took a little old house on the outskirts, the poorest shelter we ever had, with only two rooms on the floor and a loft, to which we ascended by means of a ladder. We were not discouraged, however, but managed to make the house a little genteel as well as tidy. Harriet and I used a turn-up bedstead, surrounded by pretty chintz curtains, and we made a parlor and dining room of the room by day. Harriet had a knack at twisting ribbons and fitting dresses, and she took in sewing; Catherine and Wallace went to school; and I got constant employment of a little Scotch weaver and threadmaker at twisting thread. Benjamin returned to his old place and Walker was still in the printing office."

Her little hands very early learned to contribute to the support of the family. When eleven years old she earned a dollar and twenty-five cents a week splicing rolls in a woolen factory. She says of this period: "My principal recollections are of noise and filth, bleeding hands and aching feet, and a very sad heart." Little did the residents of Eaton then dream that this little factory girl was afterward to become such an honor to their humble village. Subsequently, when she first applied for the position of teacher in the district school, a young farmer who was acting trustee, replied: "Why, the scholars will be bigger than their teacher!" But the little schoolmistress made her teaching a success, and before she was twenty years of age had contributed to the village newspaper poems of great literary merit. About this time she attracted the attention of the Misses Sheldon, who were conducting a well-known school at Utica. They offered her gratuitous instruction for a single term, and subsequently proposed to complete her education without present charge. This afforded her an excellent opportunity for self-improvement. Her health, however, had been shattered by the hardships and labors of her earlier years, and it was through great weakness and suffering that she pressed toward higher literary excellence. She was continually spurred on by her desire to secure a home for her aged parents. It was for this purpose that she wrote those charming stories, in which grace and strength of style are combined with the purest moral tone. It was under such circumstances as these that she sent to the press the stories for children, entitled "The Great Secret," "Effie Maurice," "Charles Linn,' "Allen Lucas," "John Frink," and also the fascinating tales for older readers, which were afterward gathered together under the name of " Alderbrook." Her biographer relates the following incident:

" As Miss Sheldon was at one time passing near midnight through the halls, a light streaming from Emily's apartment attracted her attention, and softly opening the door, she stole in upon her vigils. Emily sat in her night-dress, her papers lying outspread before her, grasping with both hands her throbbing temples, and pale as a marble statue. Miss S. went to her, whispered words of sympathy, and gently chided her for robbing her system of its needed repose. Emily's heart was already full, and now the fountain of feeling overflowed in uncontrollable weeping. 'Oh, Miss Sheldon,' she exclaimed, 'I *must* write! I *must* write! I must do what I can to aid my poor parents.' "

While making a visit in New York during the month of June, 1847, Miss Chubbuck wrote a letter to the " Evening Mirror," which at that time was an exceedingly popular magazine, edited by George P. Morris and N. P. Willis. In a graceful and sportive vein she offered her literary services to this periodical. This letter attracted the attention of Mr. Willis, and drew from him a characteristic reply. Mr. Willis at once introduced her through his columns to the American public, and though they saw each other but once, he became from this time on her life-long literary adviser and friend. And so, after the long struggle with poverty and ill health, this woman, by dint of an imperious will and an unmistakable genius, began to take her place among the foremost literary characters of America.

But besides her intellectual gifts, Miss Chubbuck had an intensely religious nature. She was the child of pious parents and was subject to very early religious impressions. In subsequent life she dated her conversion as occurring when she was eight years old. She used to attend all the religious services in the neighborhood. She writes:

"Indeed, I believe my solemn little face was almost ludicrously familiar to worshipers of every denomination, for I remember a Presbyterian once saying to me, as I was leaving the chapel, after having as usual asked prayers: 'What! this little girl not converted yet? How do you suppose we can waste any more time in praying for you?'" Indeed, she seems from her earliest years to have been haunted by the conviction that she was, some time or other, to be a missionary to the heathen; but she was always striving to rid herself of this irksome thought.

It was by a strange coincidence that this gifted woman, who had been from childhood deeply impressed by the story of Ann Hasseltine, should meet Mr. Judson, in January, 1846. It was at the house of Dr. Gillette in Philadelphia; Mr. Judson had been invited to come from Boston, and Dr. Gillette had gone there to bring him on. The journey was long and cold, and an accident caused a delay of three or four hours. Dr. Gillette saw in the hands of a friend a collection of light sketches called "Trippings," by Fanny Forester. He borrowed it and handed it to Mr. Judson that he might read it and so while away the tedious and uncomfortable hours of delay. Mr. Judson read portions of the book, and recognizing the power with which it was written, expressed a regret that a person of such intellectual gifts should devote them to the writing of light literature. "I should be glad to know her," he remarked. "The lady who writes so well ought to write better. It is a pity that such fine talents should be employēd on such subjects."

Dr. Gillette answered that he would soon have the pleasure of meeting her, because she was at that time a guest in his own house. Upon their arrival, Mr. Judson was entertained at the residence of Mr. Robarts, and the next morning called at Dr. Gillette's, where he met Miss Chubbuck.

This meeting began an acquaintance which ripened into an engagement, and Mr. Judson and Emily Chubbuck were married in Hamilton, N. Y., on the second of the following June. The marriage was pleasing neither to the literary nor to the religious world. The one thought that the brilliant Fanny Forester was throwing herself away in marrying "an old missionary"; the other feared that the moral grandeur of the missionary cause was compromised by an alliance between its venerable founder and a writer of fiction. These conflicting opinions made however but a slight impression upon Mr. Judson's mind. He was not dependent for his happiness and well-being upon the opinions of others. He had long before learned to think and to act independently, otherwise he would never have become a missionary, least of all a Baptist.

Less than six weeks intervened between his marriage to Miss Chubbuck and their embarkation for Burma. Many tender farewells had to be spoken. He well knew that the dear ones from whom he was parting would probably never be seen again on earth. Adoniram and Elnathan he left with Dr. and Mrs. Newton at Worcester, and his daughter Abby he committed to the care of his only sister at Plymouth.

At Boston, July 11, 1846, Mr. and Mrs. Judson, in

company with the newly appointed missionaries, Miss Lillybridge, the Beechers, and the Harrises, embarked on the "Faneuil Hall," Captain Hallett, bound for Moulmein. Many friends mingled in that farewell scene. He was leaving behind him fragrant memories. In many a household his prayers are cherished as a " precious benediction." He had been entertained in the house of his friend, Gardner Colby, of Boston, and at the family altar he thus prayed for the family of his host: " May they, and their children, and their children's children in every generation to the end of time, follow each other in uninterrupted succession through the gates of glory!" a prayer that has borne fruitage from that time until now. The Colbys came to the ship to bid him good-bye, and the Lincolns, and the Gillettes, and Mrs. Judson's bosom friend, Miss Anna Maria Anable; and among others, but dearer than all the rest, a slender youth of eighteen, the child of her who had been laid to rest at St. Helena, George Dana Boardman.

CHAPTER XII

MORE than four months elapsed after Mr. and Mrs Judson parted from their friends in Boston before they arrived at Moulmein. The passage, though long, was pleasant. In passing the Island of St. Helena his thoughts dwelt tenderly upon her who, like Rachel of old, had died "on the way, when it was but a little way to go unto Ephrath."

On the 30th of November he arrived at Moulmein, and clasped once more in his arms his little children, Henry and Edward, from whom he had parted more than eighteen months before. But, alas, one little wan face was missing! Upon his return he found that the mission at Moulmein had flourished during his absence, and was able to send an encouraging report to the corresponding secretary. But for himself he still ardently cherished the purpose to enter Burma proper. His eye was upon his old field, Rangoon. To be sure, the new Burman king was a bigoted Buddhist, and therefore bitterly opposed to the propagation of the Christian religion. But in Moulmein there were laborers enough; while in Rangoon he would be favorably situated for completing the dictionary, as he would there have access to learned men, and also to books not to be found in Moulmein. Moreover, he hoped that Burman intolerance might at last yield, and he was eager to press into the interior of the empire and establish a mission in Ava, the scene of his sufferings.

158

Impelled by these motives, Mr. and Mrs. Judson, taking with them their two little boys, embarked at Moulmein for Rangoon, on February 15, 1847. Only two months and a half had passed since their return from America. They might have been pardoned had they remained longer in the society of their missionary associates in Moulmein. But it was not their purpose to seek their own pleasure. They willingly left the twilight of Moulmein in order to penetrate the dense darkness of Rangoon, although, as Mr. Judson wrote, "it seemed harder for him to leave Moulmein for Rangoon than to leave Boston for Moulmein."

After a voyage of five days they and their two children arrived in Rangoon. Mr. Judson had previously made a visit there alone, in order "to ascertain the state of things in Burma more definitely before making an attempt to settle there." He had on that occasion hired, for fifty rupees a month, the upper part of a large brick house, which Mrs. Judson subsequently named "Bat Castle."[1] It was a place dreary indeed, and destitute of almost all outward comforts. Before engaging the house he wrote to Mrs. Judson: "The place looks as gloomy as a prison. . . . I shrink at taking you and the children into such a den, and fear you would pine and die in it." It was into this forbidding abode that he introduced the lady to whom he had been so recently married. He wrote:

"We have had a grand bat hunt to-day—bagged two hundred and fifty, and calculate to make up a round thousand before we have done."

---

[1] In a charming letter to her sister, Miss Kate Chubbuck, in whose arms she died at Hamilton, on the 1st of June, 1854, and who, the last of her family, having cared for all the rest in their sickness and declining years, was only recently laid to rest, at a good old age, by her sister's side, in the Hamilton Cemetery.

The Judsons were scarcely settled in these unpromising quarters when they learned that the house in Moulmein, where they had deposited their best clothing and most valuable goods—many of them presents from dear friends whom they were to see no more—had taken fire and had been burned to the ground with all its contents. They had brought but a few articles with them, not being willing to trust the most valuable part of their personal effects to the rapacious government at Rangoon. They had thought it best to draw their supplies from Moulmein, and now the precious consignment of articles which they had brought with them from their dear native land had been consumed in the flames. But Mr. Judson had long since mastered the science of contentment. He had been instructed both "to be full and to be hungry; both to abound and to suffer need."

Missionary operations in Rangoon were obstructed from the very outset by the intolerance of the Burmese Government. It must be remembered that the missionaries were no longer under the protection of the English flag, as they had been at Moulmein. They were exposed to the barbarities of a bigoted and unlimited despotism. The Burman monarch and his younger brother, the heir apparent, were both rigid Buddhists. And the administration of the government, though more friendly to strangers, had become more doggedly intolerant of Christianity than that of the late king. Buddhism was in full force throughout the empire, and the prospects of a missionary were never darker. The vice-governor of Rangoon, who was at that time acting governor, is described by Mr. Judson as being the most ferocious, bloodthirsty monster he had ever known in Burma. His house and courtyard resounded day and night with the screams of people under torture. It must be remembered that Mr. Judson had been received and patronized by the government, not as a missionary or propagator of religion, but as the priest of a foreign religion, ministering to the foreigners in the place.

Missionary operations, accordingly, had to be conducted with the utmost secrecy. Any known attempt at proselyting would have been instantly amenable at the criminal tribunal, and would probably have been punished by the imprisonment or death of the proselyte, and the banishment of the missionary. Nothing but a wholesome fear of the British Government kept these bloodthirsty wretches from the throat of the missionary himself. Every step was cautious, every movement slow. Mrs. Judson quietly pursued the two tasks of learning the language and writing a memorial of Mrs. Sarah Boardman Judson, which was finished during this trying period at Rangoon. Mr. Judson kept at work on the dictionary, while he gathered for secret worship the few scattered members of the native church, and the inquirers who, at the risk of imprisonment and death, visited him by night.

The condition of the missionaries in Rangoon was made still more distressing by reason of sickness. The great brick house became a hospital. One member of the family after another was prostrated by disease. Their maladies were also aggravated by the want of nourishing food. To what straits the family was reduced for food may be seen in the following sketch from Mrs. Judson's pen:

"Our milk is a mixture of buffaloes' milk, water, and something else which we cannot make out. We have changed our milk-woman several times, but it does no good. The butter we make from it is like lard with flakes

of tallow. But it is useless to write about these things—
you can get no idea. I must tell you, however, of the
grand dinner we had one day. 'You must contrive and
get something that mamma can eat,' the doctor said to
our Burmese purveyor; 'she will starve to death.'

"'What shall I get?'

"'Anything.'

"'Anything?'

"'Anything.'

"Well, we did have a capital dinner, though we tried
in vain to find out by the bones what it was. Henry said
it was *touk-tahs*, a species of lizard, and I should have
thought so too, if the little animal had been of a fleshy
consistence. Cook said he *didn't know*, but he grinned a
horrible grin which made my stomach heave a little, notwithstanding the deliciousness of the meat. In the evening we called Mr. Bazaar-man.

"'What did we have for dinner to-day?'

"'Were they good?'

"'Excellent.' A tremendous explosion of laughter,
in which the cook from his dish-room joined as loud as
he dared.

"'What were they?'

"'Rats!'

"A common servant would not have played such a
trick, but it was one of the doctor's assistants who goes
to the bazaar for us. You know the Chinese consider rats
a great delicacy, and he bought them at one of their
shops."

But amid all the discouragements and sufferings of his
life in Rangoon, Mr. Judson did not lapse into despond-
ency. At last, however, the intolerance of the government became so fierce that there was no hope of retaining

a foothold in Rangoon without going to **Ava in** order to secure the favor of the royal court.

Mr. Judson's heart was set upon this. He believed that it was the only way by which the gospel could be established in Burma proper; besides, in the completion of his dictionary, he desired to avail himself of the help of the scholars and the literature to be found only at the capital. And bitter indeed was his disappointment when the policy of retrenchment at home not only prevented his pushing on to Ava, but also compelled him to retreat from Rangoon. It was with an almost broken heart that this wise and intrepid leader, after his last fruitless effort to break the serried ranks of Burman intolerance, returned to Moulmein in obedience to the timid and narrow policy of his brethren in America. He wrote:

"It is my growing conviction that the Baptist churches in America are behind the age in missionary spirit. They now and then make a spasmodic effort to throw off a nightmare debt of some years' accumulation, and then sink back into unconscious repose. Then come paralyzing orders to retrench; new enterprises are checked in their very conception, and applicants for missionary employ are advised to wait, and soon become merged in the ministry at home. Several cases of that sort I encountered during my late visit to the United States. This state of things cannot last always. The Baptist missions will probably pass into the hands of other denominations, or be temporarily suspended; and those who have occupied the van will fall back into the rear. Nebuchadnezzar will be driven out from men, to eat grass like an ox, until seven times pass over him. But he will, at length, recover his senses, and be restored to the throne of his kingdom, and reign over the whole earth."

Two years afterward, only a few months before his death, he received permission from the Board to go to Ava.

But this permission came too late. The opportunity of penetrating Burma proper had passed, and the aid of an excellent Burmese scholar, once a priest at Ava, had been secured at Moulmein. Thus, after spending half a year of toil and suffering at Rangoon, he was compelled to fall back upon Moulmein. He arrived there with his family on September 5, 1847.

During this experience of repulse, occasioned by the inertness of Christians at home, it would have consoled him could he have foreseen that the very point which he so ardently desired to reach and occupy, would subsequently become the site of a vigorous native church, and that a beautiful house of worship would be erected as his monument in the heart of the Burman empire at Mandalay, to which the capital has been transferred from old Ava, only a few miles distant.

His wife, in one of her letters, thus describes his indefatigable industry:

"The good man works like a galley slave, and really it quite distresses me sometimes; but he seems to get fat on it, so I try not to worry. He walks—or rather *runs*—like a boy over the hills, a mile or two every morning; then down to his books, scratch-scratch, puzzle-puzzle, and when he gets deep in the mire, out on the veranda with your humble servant by his side, walking and talking (*kan-ing* we call it in the Burman) till the point is elucidated, and then down again; and so on till ten o'clock in the evening. It is this *walking* which is keeping him out of the grave."

At the same time he took a general oversight of the

mission work in Moulmein, being, in the nature of the
case, a guiding and inspiring force. He preached occasionally in the native chapel, "one sermon, at least, every
Lord's Day." When his beloved fellow-missionary, Mr.
Haswell, was compelled to return home for a short visit
on account of his ill health, the whole care of the native
church devolved on him.

These literary and pastoral labors were, however, light-
ened by social and domestic pleasures. Though he had
come to the ripe age of sixty, he had within him the fresh
heart of a boy. It has been truly said of him that his
spirit was intensely, unconquerably youthful. He loved
to romp with his children, and early in the morning to
brush

> With hasty steps the dew away

In a life of self-sacrifice he had discovered the peren-
nial fountain of joy. While he followed the narrow path
of stern duty, the butterfly pleasure which the worldling
chases from flower to flower had flown into his bosom.
Byron, on his thirty-ninth birthday, breathed the sigh:

> My days are in the yellow leaf,
> The flower and fruits of life are gone;
> The worm, the canker, and the grief
> Are mine alone.

How different Judson's words uttered on his death-bed.
"I suppose they think me an old man, and imagine it
is nothing for one like me to resign a life so full of trials.
But I am not old—at least in that sense; you know I
am not. Oh, no man ever left the world with more in-
viting prospects, with brighter hopes, or warmer feelings—warmer feelings."

We are indebted for the following description of his

personal appearance at this time to Dr. Wayland's memoir:

"In person, Dr. Judson was of about the medium height, slenderly built, but compactly knitted together. His complexion was in youth fair; but residence in India had given him the sallow hue common to that climate. His hair, when in this country, was yet of a fine chestnut, with scarcely a trace of gray. The elasticity of his movement indicated a man of thirty, rather than of nearly sixty years of age. His deportment was, in a remarkable degree, quiet and self-possessed, and his manner was pointed out as perfectly well-bred by those who consider the cultivation of social accomplishments the serious business of life. A reviewer writes on this subject as follows:

"'A person overtaking Judson in one of his early morning walks, as he strode along the pagoda-capped hills of Moulmein, would have thought the pedestrian before him rather under-sized, and of a build showing no great muscular development; although the pace was good and the step firm, yet there was nothing to indicate great powers of physical endurance in the somewhat slight and spare frame tramping steadily in front of the observer. The latter would scarcely suppose that he had before him the man who, on the 25th of March, 1826, wrote: "Through the kind interposition of our Heavenly Father, our lives have been preserved in the most imminent danger from the hand of the executioner, and in repeated instances of most alarming illness, during my protracted imprisonment of one year and seven months; nine months in three pairs of fetters, two months in five, six months in one, and two months a prisoner at large." Illness nigh unto death, and three or five pairs of fetters to aid in weighing down the shattered and exhausted frame, seemed a dispensation calculated for the endurance of a far more muscular build. But meet the man, instead of overtaking him; or, better still, see him enter a room and bare his head, and the observer at once caught an eye beaming with intelligence, a countenance full of life and expression. Attention could scarcely fail of being riveted on that head and face, which told at once that the spiritual and intellectual formed the man; the physical was wholly subordinate, and must have been borne through its trials by the more essential elements of the individual, by the *feu sacré* which predominated in his disposition. Nor was this impression weakened by his conversation. Wisdom and piety were, as might be expected in such a man, its general tone; but there was a vivacity pervading it which indicated strong, buoyant, though well, it may be said very severely, disciplined animal spirits. Wit too was there, playful, pure, free from malice, and a certain quiet Cervantic humor, full of benignity, would often enliven and illustrate what he had to say on purely temporal affairs.'"

To his fellow-missionaries his wide experience and affectionate disposition made him an invaluable adviser and friend. When they found themselves in trouble and sorrow they were sure to receive from his lips words of comfort and counsel. The great pressure of his public cares and other labors did not make him moody or absent-minded at home. His love for his children was deep and tender, as attested by his exquisite letters to his daughter, Abby, who was living at Bradford in the old homestead of the Hasseltine family, and to his boys, Adoniram and Elnathan, who were pursuing their studies in Worcester.

The two little boys who formed a part of the family group at Moulmein, often found in their father an ardent companion in their play. One of them well remembers how his father used to come into his room in the morning and greet him upon his first awakening with a delicious piece of Burmese cake, or with the joyful tidings that a rat had been caught in the trap the night before. He wrote to Mr. Stevens in Rangoon:

"I have to hold a meeting with the rising generation every evening, and that takes time. Henry can say, 'Twinkle, twinkle,' all himself, and Edward can repeat it after his father! Giants of genius! paragons of erudition!"

On December 24, 1847, Emily Frances Judson[1] was born at Moulmein. The happy mother addressed to her infant the following exquisite lines, which have been since treasured in so many hearts throughout the world:

MY BIRD.

Ere last year's moon had left the sky
  A birdling sought my Indian nest,
And folded, O, so lovingly!   *
  Her tiny wings upon my breast.

From morn till evening's purple tinge
  In winsome helplessness she lies;
Two rose leaves, with a silken fringe,
  Shut softly on her starry eyes. .

There's not in Ind a lovelier bird;
  Broad earth owns not a happier nest;
O God, thou hast a fountain stirred,
  Whose waters never more shall rest!

This beautiful, mysterious thing,
  This seeming visitant from heaven—

---

[1] Now the wife of the Rev. T. A. T. Hanna, Pottsville, Pa.

This bird with the immortal wing,
  To me—to me, thy hand hath given.

The pulse first caught its tiny stroke,
  The blood its crimson hue from mine;
This life, which I have dared invoke,
  Henceforth is parallel with thine.

A silent awe is in my room;
  I tremble with delicious fear;
The future with its light and gloom,—
  Time and eternity are here.

Doubts—hopes, in eager tumult rise;
  Hear, O my God! one earnest prayer:
Room for my bird in paradise,
  And give her angel-plumage there!

But dark shadows began to gather around the path of the missionary. Soon after the birth of Emily, Mrs. Judson's health began perceptibly to decline and to cause him doleful forebodings. Little did he imagine that in the journey through the valley of the shadow of death, he was to precede his wife by several years. In November, 1849, he was attacked by the disease which, after a period of a little over four months, culminated in his death. One night, while sharing with Mrs. Judson the care of one of the children who had been taken suddenly ill, he caught a severe cold. This settled on his lungs and produced a terrible cough with some fever. After three or four days, he was attacked with dysentery, and before this was subdued a congestive fever set in, from which he never recovered. A trip down the coast of Mergui afforded only partial relief. He tried the sea at Amherst, but only sank the more rapidly, and then hastened back to Moulmein. The following is his last communication to the Board:

MOULMEIN, February 21, 1850.

" *To the Corresponding Secretary.*

"MY DEAR BROTHER :—I cannot manage a pen, so please excuse pencil. I have been prostrated with fever ever since the latter part of last November, and have suffered so much that I have frequently remarked that I was never ill in India before. Through the mercy of God, I think I am convalescent for the last ten days; but the doctor and all my friends are very urgent that I should take a sea voyage of a month or two, and be absent from here a long time. May God direct in the path of duty. My hand is failing, so I will beg to remain

" Yours affectionately,

" A. JUDSON."

His only hope now lay in a long sea voyage. He was never so happy as when upon the ocean. The salt breezes had never failed to invigorate him. But it was a sore trial to part with his wife and children when there was but little prospect of ever seeing them again.

There was, however, no alternative. A French bark, the " Aristide Marie," was to sail from Moulmein on the 3d of April. The dying missionary was carried on board by his weeping disciples, accompanied only by Mr. Ranney, of the Moulmein mission. There were unfortunate delays in going down the river, so that several days were lost. Meantime that precious life was ebbing rapidly away. It was not until Monday the 8th, that the vessel got out to sea. Then came head winds and sultry weather, and after four days and nights of intense agony, Mr. Judson breathed his last on the 12th of April, 1850, and on the same day his body was buried in the sea, without a prayer. He died within a week from the time that he parted with his wife, and almost four months of terrible suspense elapsed before she learned of his death. The tidings were sent to her by the Rev. Dr. Mackay, a Scotch Presbyterian minister of Calcutta. Who can fathom her experience of suffering during those weary months of waiting! On the 22d of April, within three weeks of the time when she said farewell to her husband, exactly ten days after his body, without her knowledge, had found its resting-place in the sea, she gave birth to a second child; whom she named Charles for her father. But the same day his little spirit, as though unwilling to linger amid such scenes of desolation, took its upward flight to be forever united with the parent who had entered the gates of paradise only a little in advance.

CHAPTER XIII

MR. JUDSON did not live to complete the Burmese dictionary. He finished the English and Burmese part, but the Burmese and English was left in an unfinished state. In accordance with his desire, expressed only a few days before his death, Mrs. Judson transmitted his manuscripts to his trusted friend and associate in missionary toil, Mr. Stevens, upon whom accordingly the task of completing the work devolved.

During the long winter of our Northern States sometimes a mass of snow accumulates, little by little, in the corner of the farmer's meadow. Under the warm rays of the spring sun the dazzling bank gradually melts away, but leaves upon the greensward, which it has sheltered, a fertilizing deposit. It now remains for us to ask what stimulating residuum this great life which we have attempted to describe left behind it upon the surface of human society.

Mr. Judson's achievements far transcended the wildest aspirations of his youth. During the early years in Rangoon, when the mighty purpose of evangelizing Burma began to take definite shape in his mind; even before the first convert, Moung Nau, was baptized; when, indeed, the young missionary was almost forgotten by his fellow-Christians at home, or merely pitied as a good-hearted enthusiast, the outermost limit reached by his strong-winged hope was that he might, before he died, build up

172

a church of a hundred converted Burmans, and translate the whole Bible into their language.   But far more than this was accomplished during the ten years in Rangoon, the two years in Ava, and the twenty-three years in Moulmein.   At the time of his death the native Christians (Burmans and Karens publicly baptized upon the profession of their faith) numbered over seven thousand. Besides this, hundreds throughout Burma had died rejoicing in the Christian faith.   He had not only finished, the translation of the Bible, but had accomplished the larger and the more difficult part of the compilation of a Burmese dictionary.   At the time of his death there were sixty-three churches established among the Burmans and Karens.   These churches were under the oversight of one hundred and sixty-three missionaries, native pastors, and assistants.   He had laid the foundations of Christianity deep down in the Burman heart, where they could never be swept away.

This achievement is the more startling when we consider that all divine operations are slow in the beginning, but rush to the consummation with lightning speed. Many long days elapse while the icy barriers are being slowly loosened beneath the breath of spring.   But at last the freshet comes, and the huge frozen masses are broken up and carried rapidly to the sea.   The leaves slowly ripen for the grave.   Though withered, they still cling to the boughs.   But finally a day comes in the autumn when suddenly the air is full of falling foliage. It takes a long time for the apple to reach its growth, but a very brief time suffices for the ripening.   Tennyson's lark

> Shook his song together as he neared
> His happy home, the ground.

Nature is instinct with this law, and we may well believe that though the processes are slow and inconspicuous by which the ancient structures of false religions are being undermined, yet the time will come when they will tumble suddenly into ruins; when a nation shall be converted in a day; when, "As earth bringeth forth her bud and as the garden causeth the things that are sown in it to spring forth, so the Lord will cause righteousness and praise to spring forth before all the nations." In the baptism of ten thousand Telugus in India within a single year, do we not already see the gray dawn of such an era of culmination?

> We are living, we are dwelling
>   In a grand and awful time;
> In an age on ages telling,
>   To be living is sublime.
> Hark! the waking up of nations,
>   Gog and Magog to the fray.
> Hark! what soundeth? 'Tis creation
>   Groaning for its latter day.

But it was Mr. Judson's lot to labor in the hard and obscure period of the first beginnings. And not only so, but he undertook the task of planting Christianity not among a people like the Sandwich Islanders, without literature and without an elaborate religious system, but rather in a soil already pre-occupied by an ancient classical literature and by a time-honored ritual, which now numbers among its devotees one-third of the population of our globe.

When these considerations are taken into account, the tangible results which Mr. Judson left behind at his death seem simply amazing. But these are only a small part of what he really accomplished. Being dead, he yet speaketh. The Roman Church has preserved an old legend that John, the beloved disciple, "did not die at all, but is only slumbering, and moving the grave mound with his breath until the final return of the Lord." And in a sense it is true that a great man does not die. You cannot bury a saint so deep that he will not move those who walk over his grave. The upheavals of society are mainly due to the breath of those who have vanished from the earth and lie beneath its bosom.

The early action of Mr. Judson and his fellow-students at Andover resulted in the formation of the American Board of Commissioners for Foreign Missions. This society, representing the Congregationalists of this country, may justly claim to be the mother of American foreign missionary bodies. It was organized for the support of certain young men while they were engaged in the work to which the Lord called them. Institutions, according to Emerson, are the lengthened shadows of individual men. Societies do not call men into being, but men create societies. The society is only a convenient vehicle through which the Christian at home can send bread to the missionary abroad, whose whole time is devoted to feeding the heathen with the bread of life.

In the year 1892, the American Board of Commissioners for Foreign Missions received and expended eight hundred and forty-one thousand dollars. It is conducting successful missionary operations in Africa, Turkey, India, China, Japan, Micronesia, the Hawaiian Islands, Mexico, Spain, and Austria. In these different countries it has four hundred and forty-four churches, forty-one thousand five hundred and twenty-two church-members, and three thousand two hundred and ninety-eight missionaries, native pastors, teachers, and assistants.

The change in Mr. Judson's views on the subject of baptism led almost immediately to the formation of a Baptist Missionary Society, now known as the American Baptist Missionary Union. During the year ending May 1, 1893, there passed through the treasury of this Society seven hundred and sixty-six thousand, seven hundred and eighty-two dollars and ninety-five cents, given by the Baptists of the United States for the evangelization of the heathen. This society is at work in Burma, Siam, India, China, Japan, Africa, and also in the countries of Europe, and it reported, in 1893, one thousand five hundred and thirty-one churches, over one hundred and sixty-nine thousand church-members, eighty-five thousand six hundred and eighty-four Sunday-school scholars, as well as two thousand and seventy preachers.

A few years after Mr. Judson's departure from this country, and organization of these two societies, the Episcopalians and also the Methodists of America organized for the work of foreign missions. For many years the Presbyterians joined the Congregationalists, and poured their contributions into the treasury of the American Board. But in 1836 they organized a society, now known as the Board of Foreign Missions of the Presbyterian Church. Its fields of operation are Syria, Persia, Japan, China, Siam, India, Africa, South America, Central America, and Mexico, with an expenditure in 1893 of one million sixty-three thousand six hundred and forty-five dollars and sixty-five cents. It supports two thousand two hundred and seventy missionaries and lay missionaries, and reports three hundred and ninety-eight churches with thirty-one thousand three hundred and twenty-four communicants, and twenty-eight thousand nine hundred and eighty-three scholars in the native schools.

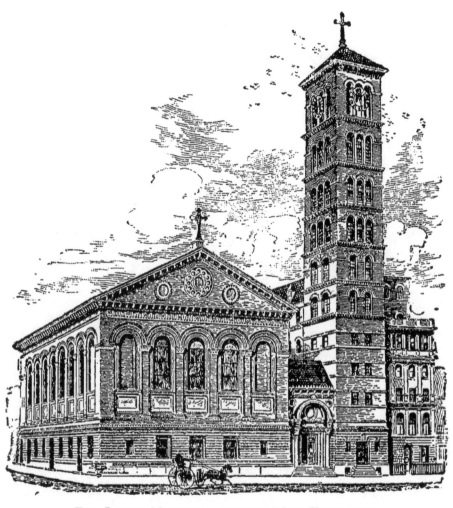

THE JUDSON MEMORIAL CHURCH, NEW YORK CITY.

Adoniram Judson.   Page 177.

All these vigorous Christian societies, sustained by the missionary conviction of the churches in America, with their vast army of missionaries and native communicants now pressing against the systems of heathenism at a thousand points, when they come to tell the story of their origin do not fail to make mention of the name of Adoniram Judson. His life formed a part of the fountain-head from which flow these beneficent streams which fringe with verdure the wastes of paganism.

And in other lands than America has Mr. Judson's career of heroic action and suffering proved an inspiration to churches of every name.

But not only in the foreign mission enterprise has the power of his example been felt. Work among the heathen is sure to react upon Christians at home, and impel them to work for the heathen at their doors. The missionary spirit is all one, within foreign parts or on Western prairies or in the slums of our great towns. A zeal which is not deaf to the cry of the perishing millions in China and Africa can be relied upon for continuous effort in home mission work. A rifle which can be depended upon at a thousand yards will not fail you when fired point-blank. It is not unfitting that in New York a monument should rise to Adoniram Judson, suggestive of the organic unity of Foreign Missions, Home Missions, and City Missions.

There are very few of those who have gone from this country as missionaries to the heathen who are not indebted to Mr. Judson for methods and inspiration. The writer will not soon forget a scene he witnessed at Saratoga in May, 1880. The General Assembly of the Presbyterian Church was in session. Dr. Jessup, an eminent missionary in Syria, then on a visit to this country, had been elected moderator. When the session of the Assembly had ended, he entered the convention which the Baptists were then holding also in Saratoga. As an honored guest he was invited to speak. There was a breathless silence through the house as the veteran missionary arose, and with inspiring words urged the prosecution of the missionary enterprise. He closed by saying that when he should arrive in heaven the first person whose hand he desired to grasp next to the Apostle Paul would be Adoniram Judson.

A life which embodies Christ's idea of complete self-abnegation cannot but become a great object lesson. A man cannot look into the mirror of such a career without becoming at once conscious of his own selfishness and of the triviality of a merely worldly life. A New York merchant in his boyhood read Wayland's "Life of Judson," and laying the book down left his chamber, went out into the green meadow belonging to his father's farm, and consecrated his young life to the service of God.

How many unknown souls have been attracted to Christ by the same magnetism! How many others have been lifted out of their self-love! How many have been drawn toward the serener heights of Christian experience by the example of him whose strong aspirings after holiness are depicted in " The Threefold Cord "! Oh, that some young man might rise from the reading of these memoirs and lay down his life in all its freshness and strength upon the altar of God, so that he might become like Paul of old, a chosen vessel of Christ to bear his name before the Gentiles and kings and the children of Israel!

The memory of Mr. Judson's sufferings in Ava will never cease to nerve missionary endeavor. They appeared at the time unnecessary and fruitless. He himself, upon emerging from them, spoke of them as having been "unavailing to answer any valuable missionary purpose unless so far as they may have been silently blessed to our spiritual improvement and capacity for future usefulness." But the spectacle of our missionary lying in an Oriental prison, his ankles freighted with five pairs of irons, his heroic wife ministering to him like an angel during the long months of agony, has burned itself into the consciousness of Christendom, and has made retreat from the missionary enterprise an impossibility. It is God's law that progress should be along the line of suffering. The world's benefactors have been its sufferers. They "have been from time immemorial crucified and burned."[1] It seems to be a divine law that those who pluck and bestow roses must feel thorns. The sufferings of Mr. Judson's life were as fruitful of blessing as the toils.

The graves of the sainted dead forbid retreat from the ramparts of heathenism. It is said that the heart of the Scottish hero, Bruce, was embalmed after his death and preserved in a silver casket. When his descendants were making a last desperate charge upon the serried columns of the Saracens, their leader threw this casket far out into the ranks of the enemy, crying "Forward, heart of Bruce!" The Scots charged with irresistible fury in order to regain the heart of their dead king. Into the thick of heathenism noble men have penetrated and fallen there. Christianity will never retreat from the graves of its dead heroes. England is pressing into Africa with redoubled energy since she saw placed on the pavement of her own Westminister Abbey the marble

[1] Goethe.

tablet bearing the words: "Brought by faithful hands, over land and sea, David Livingstone, missionary, traveler, philanthropist." Until that day shall come when every knee shall bow and every tongue confess the name of Jesus, Christian hearts will not cease to draw inspiration from the memory of those who found their last resting-places under the hopia-tree at Amherst, on the rocky shore of St. Helena, and beneath the stormy breast of the Indian Ocean.

LITERATURE

MEMOIR. By REV. Francis Wayland, D. D. Two Vols. 12mo. Boston, 1853.

MEMOIR. By J. Clement. 12mo. Auburn, N. Y., 1852.

RECORDS OF LIFE, CHARACTER, AND ACHIEVEMENTS OF ADONIRAM JUDSON. By Rev. D. F. Middleditch. 12mo. New York, 1854.

THE EARNEST MAN: A SKETCH OF THE CHARACTER AND LABORS OF THE REV. ADONIRAM JUDSON. By Mrs. H. C. Conant. 8vo. Boston, 1856.

ANN HASSELTINE JUDSON. By Rev. James D. Knowles. Boston, 1829. (Many times reprinted.)

SARAH BOARDMAN JUDSON. By Mrs. Emily C. Judson. 18mo. New York, 1850.

EMILY CHUBBUCK JUDSON. By Dr. A. C. Kendrick. 12mo. New York, 1860.

THE LIVES OF THE THREE MRS. JUDSONS. By Mrs. A. M. Wilson. New York, 1851–55.

MISSIONARY MEMORIALS: ANN H.; SARAH B.; AND EMILY C. JUDSON. By W. N. Wyeth, D. D. Philadelphia, 1894.

LITERARY WORKS OF DR. JUDSON

TRANSLATION OF THE BIBLE INTO BURMESE: THE AC-
CEPTED VERSION.

ENGLISH AND BURMAN DICTIONARY. Completed by Mr.
Stevens.

GRAMMATICAL NOTICES OF THE BURMAN LANGUAGE.

A VIEW OF THE CHRISTIAN RELIGION IN THREE PARTS.
HISTORIC, DIDACTIC, AND PRECEPTIVE.

VARIOUS TRACTS AND PAMPHLETS.

GENERAL INDEX

185

186 INDEX

NOTABLE BAPTISTS.

A series of short, popular Baptist biographies. 12mo., 192 pp. Price, 90 cts.

I. ADONIRAM JUDSON.
By his son, Edward Judson, D. D.
Published.

II. ANDREW FULLER.
By Robert S. MacArthur, D. D.
In preparation.

III. JAMES MANNING.
By E. Benj. Andrews, LL. D.
In preparation.

IV. RICHARD FULLER.
By J. L. M. Curry, LL. D.
In preparation.

V. FRANCIS WAYLAND.

Others will be provided for from time to time.